Post Carbon Cities:
Planning for Energy and Climate Uncertainty

A Guidebook on Peak Oil and Global Warming for Local Governments

DANIEL LERCH
POST CARBON INSTITUTE

Post Carbon Cities: Planning for Energy and Climate Uncertainty
by Daniel Lerch

Copyright © 2007 by Post Carbon Institute
All rights reserved
Design: Grapheon Communications Design
Cover Photo: Reimar Gaertner

Published by Post Carbon Press
1st printing August 2007; 2nd printing April 2008
Printed in the United States of America
Printed on 60% recycled paper

ISBN-13: 978-0-9767510-5-2
ISBN-10: 0-9767510-5-4

Order online at
www.postcarbonbooks.com

Post Carbon Press
Sebastopol, California, USA
www.postcarbonpress.com

www.postcarbon.org

Table of Contents

Executive Summary v

Energy and climate uncertainty v

Incentives to act locally vi

Four initial steps vi

Five principles for the long term vii

Join the conversation online vii

Foreword viii

Preface ix

What is this guidebook? ix

Who should use this guidebook, and why? ix

About the Author ix

Post Carbon Cities program ix

About Post Carbon Institute x

Acknowledgements x

1. Introduction 1

1.1. The new challenge of uncertainty 1

1.2. Peak oil and energy uncertainty 2

A changing world 2

A big problem 2

1.3. Global warming and climate uncertainty 3

1.4. A job for government 3

1.5. A job for municipalities 4

1.6. Planning for energy and climate uncertainty 5

1.7. Urgency to act 5

2. The End of Cheap Oil and Natural Gas 7

2.1. Uses of oil and natural gas 8

2.2. Oil supply and demand 9

Oil flow: the real issue 10

Oil production: the realities of long term decline 11

2.3. Natural gas supply and demand 14

2.4. Unconventional oil and substitutes 14

2.5. The implications 17

Oil and gas price volatility 17

Won't the global economy respond? 17

3. Local Challenges, Local Advantages 21

3.1. The challenges our cities face 21

What are the most urgent vulnerabilities? 22

3.2. Understanding the complexity of energy uncertainty 22

Overlapping, intertwined issues 22

High oil prices, higher asphalt prices 25

3.3. Responding at the local level 27

Why municipal action? 27

The advantages of the local level 27

3.4. Reaching out beyond City Hall 29

Local context 29

State/Provincial and regional context 30

National context 32

3.5. Leadership 32

Leadership within local government 33

Leadership for complexity 33

4. Responses to Energy and Climate Uncertainty **37**

   4.1. Local government responses to energy uncertainty 37

      Metropolitan Region Case Study: Portland, Oregon 39

      Medium-sized City Case Study: Hamilton, Ontario 44

      Smaller City Case Study: Willits, California 46

      Summary of other cities' actions 47

      Lessons Learned 50

   4.2. Local government responses to climate uncertainty 51

      Mitigation 52

      Adaptation and Next Steps 55

5. Transitioning to the Post Carbon World **59**

   5.1. Unprecedented challenges 59

   5.2. Unusual opportunities 60

   5.3. What your city can do 61

      Post Carbon Cities: Four Initial Steps 62

      Post Carbon Cities: Five Principles 63

   5.4. The Bottom Line 67

Appendix **69**

   Making a government statement on peak oil 70

   Establishing a peak oil task force 73

   Systems Thinking: A Tool for Municipalities 79

   Resources 85

   Endnotes 91

   Photo credits 95

Index **97**

Boxes

   Box 1. Mixed views on the future of oil 13

   Box 2. The U.S. Department of Energy "Hirsch Report" on peak oil 18

   Box 3. Local Impacts and Vulnerabilities, Portland (Ore.) Peak Oil Task Force 23

   Box 4. Energy and land use / transportation planning 24

   Box 5. Oil prices and street maintenance costs 26

   Box 6. Learning from related approaches 34

   Box 7. Portland (Ore.) Peak Oil Task Force Recommendations 43

   Box 8. Sebastopol (Calif.) Citizens Advisory Group on Energy
      Vulnerability Recommendations 48

   Box 9. ICLEI's Cities for Climate Protection Campaign 53

   Box 10. U.S. Mayors Climate Protection Agreement 54

   Box 11. Adapting to Global Warming: Impacts and Policy 56

   Box 12. Adapting to Global Warming: Local Functions 57

   Box 13. "Wedge" strategies 64

   Box 14. San Francisco (Calif.) Peak Oil Resolution 71

Executive Summary

Post Carbon Cities: Planning for Energy and Climate Uncertainty **provides guidance and support to local government officials and staff for meeting three critical goals: breaking community dependence on oil, stopping community contributions to global warming, and preparing the community to thrive in a time of energy and climate uncertainty.**

The most direct strategy for achieving these goals is to ***reduce consumption*** and ***produce locally:*** reduce the community's overall resource consumption, and develop the capacity of local farmers and manufacturers to provide for the community's basic needs. The more your community can get its energy, food and other basic goods from local sources, the less vulnerable it will be to rising and volatile energy prices, and the less it will contribute to climate change.

Energy and climate uncertainty Most credible observers now recognize that our global climate faces radical change in the coming decades if we do not take immediate and far-reaching action. Peak oil (the coming high point and subsequent decline of world oil production) is not as widely understood, but presents a similarly complex set of challenges.

Time is short to prepare for peak oil and global warming. At current rates of fossil fuel consumption we will most likely pass peak oil by 2010*, and we seriously risk widespread, catastrophic climate change if we do not begin dramatically reducing global carbon emissions.†

The key problem posed by both peak oil and global warming is ultimately one of *uncertainty*: these phenomena are creating changes that we cannot easily predict in economies and ecosystems at the global, regional and even local levels. For local governments — responsible for managing local public services, planning for future land use and transportation, and protecting the community's economic and social health— this uncertainty creates a wide variety of risks and vulnerabilities. How will local economies be affected when the price of oil passes $200 a barrel? How will regional climate shifts affect local water supplies? Local government decision-makers need to understand and respond to these challenges.

> **Peak oil and global warming are creating changes in economies and ecosystems that we cannot easily predict.**

Executive Summary

Just about everything you do to reduce energy consumption and carbon emissions in your community will save money in the long run.

Incentives to act locally   As many southeastern U.S. municipalities discovered after Hurricane Katrina knocked out regional fuel pipelines in 2005, state/provincial and federal government agencies do not have the ability to meet every jurisdiction's resource needs in times of crisis. Local governments, however, have the flexibility, capacity and motivation to address risk management and emergency response needs in ways that higher-level government agencies cannot.

Local governments also have strong financial incentives to address peak oil and climate change. Reducing local oil dependence and carbon emissions means pursuing energy-efficient buildings, locally-controlled energy sources, compact transit-oriented land uses, alternative transportation modes and other aims that are energy prudent, and thus ultimately fiscally conservative. When the challenges created by peak oil and climate change are not future risks but present problems, those communities that have prepared will have distinct advantages over those that haven't.

Additionally, local governments are well-positioned to address peak oil and climate change because they have influence over three key areas of urban spatial and economic development:

- **Building construction and energy efficiency.** Through zoning codes, building codes and the permitting process, municipalities can encourage building designs that save energy and resources.

- **Local land use and transportation patterns.** Municipal land use and transportation planning decisions directly influence whether people and businesses will have mobility choices that allow them to save energy and money.

- **Local economic activity.** Municipal economic development initiatives are opportunities to encourage development in low-energy, zero-carbon directions, by both incentive and example.

Four Initial Steps   Over the last fifteen years, hundreds of local governments in the U.S. and Canada have begun systematically reducing their greenhouse gas emissions in response to global warming. And since 2004, when oil prices climbed beyond 15-year highs, a growing number of local and regional government agencies in both countries have begun responding to the threats posed by peak oil.

Drawing from the experiences of these cities, here are **four initial steps** that your own community can take to address peak oil and global warming.

1: Sign the U.S. Mayors Climate Protection Agreement / Endorse the World Mayors and Municipal Leaders Declaration on Climate Change. For U.S. mayors, signing the Climate Protection Agreement commits your city to greenhouse gas reduction in the absence of federal leadership. Both U.S. and Canadian cities can also contribute to international carbon mitigation efforts by signing the Declaration on Climate Change. See www.coolmayors.com and www.iclei.org/montrealsummit.

2: Join ICLEI's Cities for Climate Protection Campaign[†] to get your city started on reducing energy use and greenhouse gas emissions, and to connect to the resources and expertise of the leading global movement of local governments working on climate change. See www.iclei.org.

3: Sign the Oil Depletion Protocol, which sets a target for reducing oil consumption across your community. Signing the Protocol sends a signal to citizens, business leaders and municipal staff that your city is serious about reducing its energy vulnerability. See www.oildepletionprotocol.org.

4: Establish a Peak Oil Task Force to quickly identify the challenges and vulnerabilities your community faces as a result of peak oil. A task force is also a valuable way to introduce community stakeholders to the challenges of energy uncertainty, and engage them in developing a broad-based response. See *Appendix: Establishing a peak oil task force.*

Five principles for the long term

Integrate these **five principles** into your local government's decision-making and planning processes to comprehensively address energy and climate uncertainty over the long term:

1. Deal with transportation and land use (or you may as well stop now). Fundamentally rethink your municipality's land use and transportation practices, from building and zoning codes to long-range planning. Make land use and transportation planning decisions with 100-year timeframes. Organize with neighboring jurisdictions to address the land use and transportation challenges of energy and climate uncertainty at a regional level.

2. Tackle private energy consumption. Use the tools you already have to encourage serious energy conservation and efficiency in the private sector. Engage the business community aggressively, challenging your local business leaders to reinvent the local economy for the post-carbon world.

3. Attack the problems piece-by-piece and from many angles. Meet your energy and climate uncertainty response goals with multiple, proven solutions, pursuing many different kinds of solutions at different scales. Enlist the entire community, setting clear community goals and spurring action from all sides to meet them.

4. Plan for fundamental changes... and make fundamental changes happen. Educate and involve your fellow elected officials, staff and community stakeholders about energy and climate uncertainty, challenging them to come up with serious solutions. Lead your city's transition by integrating peak oil and climate change considerations into your own decision-making.

5. Build a sense of community. In short, do anything you can to get people talking with each other, forming relationships, and investing themselves in the larger community.

Join the conversation online
The Post Carbon Cities program of Post Carbon Institute helps local governments address the challenges posed by peak oil and global warming, providing resources for elected officials and staff to develop responses appropriate to their communities. Please visit us online at www.postcarboncities.net and join the growing movement of local leaders who are preparing their communities for the challenges of energy and climate uncertainty.

Visit Post Carbon Cities online for more resources on responding to peak oil and global warming.

---

* According to an increasing number of petroleum analysts, we seem to be facing an undulating plateau of world oil production from 2007 onward, with permanent decline likely underway by 2010. See page 12.

† In 2006 James Hansen, director of NASA's Goddard Institute for Space Studies, publicly called for immediate, broad-based action to reduce carbon emissions, saying "we have a very brief window of opportunity to deal with climate change...no longer than a decade, at the most."

‡ The ICLEI (International Council for Local Environmental Initiatives) Cities for Climate Protection program works with cities around the world to track and reduce local greenhouse gas emissions. In Canada, this program is implemented for ICLEI by the Federation of Canadian Municipalities as "Partners for Climate Change"; see http://www.iclei.org.

Foreword

by Julian Darley, President of Post Carbon Institute

In just the last year it's become widely accepted that global warming and the peaking of global oil production together pose unprecedented challenges for modern industrial civilization. This broad political and cultural shift—especially in the United States—comes not a moment too soon. Since the first printing of *Post Carbon Cities: Planning for Energy and Climate Uncertainty*, oil prices have broken through the previous record set in 1980 to settle at unprecedented highs, and two major new studies suggest that we have already exceeded the safe upper limit of atmospheric carbon dioxide concentrations.

Fortunately, more and more American and Canadian local governments are responding decisively to peak oil and global warming. We're now seeing cities from British Columbia to Texas to Vermont convene peak oil task forces and draw up contingency plans, and the number of cities developing climate change mitigation and adaptation plans is expanding with extraordinary rapidity. Just as important, energy and climate issues are clearly becoming mainstream. Relatively conservative Spokane, Washington recently became the first city in the U.S. (and one of the first in the world) to convene a task force explicitly addressing peak oil and global warming together.

Post Carbon Institute's mission is to help society make the transition to a post-carbon world: a world that is no longer dependent on hydrocarbon fuels nor emitting climate-changing levels of carbon. We take a pragmatic and research-based approach to peak oil and global warming, both in understanding the complexities of the challenges we face and in developing systemic and powerful responses to them. We analyze the roles that key inputs like fossil fuels, solar energy and water play in our ecological, economic and social systems. We ask where leverage points and possible levers of power are, and how we can use them to further our mission.

It is this broad-thinking, results-based focus that informs Post Carbon Institute's varied programs, all aimed at helping communities understand and respond to the energy and global sustainability challenges we face in the 21st century. We work with citizens through our Relocalization Network of nearly 200 grassroots groups, and we work with local governments through our Post Carbon Cities program for elected officials and planning professionals. We report on and disseminate hard-to-find information about peak oil and relocalization through our Global Public Media internet broadcasting channel, and we turn ideas into replicable action with our Energy Farm and Solar CarShare programs. At both the international and local levels we promote the Oil Depletion Protocol to voluntarily reduce government, business and household dependence on declining global oil supplies.

Post Carbon Cities: Planning for Energy and Climate Uncertainty has quickly become a valuable and sought-after resource for professionals and laypersons alike, with some government agencies buying the book in bulk to distribute to staff. Author Daniel Lerch is now recognized as a leading authority on local government responses to peak oil; he presents regularly to city councils, planning departments and conferences throughout the U.S., with major recent events in Canada, Ireland and the U.K.

We're excited and proud that *Post Carbon Cities* has emerged as the leading resource for communities that want not only to survive but to thrive in the new world of energy and climate uncertainty. We hope this book will serve you well, and that you'll add your own community's experiences to the resources and discussions at www.postcarboncities.net.

Sebastopol, California
April 2008

Preface

What is this guidebook?

Post Carbon Cities: Planning for Energy and Climate Uncertainty is a guidebook for local governments on "peak oil" (the moment at which global oil production hits its highest point, followed by a permanent decline) and global warming. It provides a sober look at the challenges that peak oil and global warming are creating for local governments, and explains what local decision-makers can do to address these challenges.

The Guidebook is divided into six sections:

Section 1 Introduction describes how peak oil and global warming are creating a new problem of energy and climate uncertainty, and what this means for local governments.

Section 2 The End of Cheap Oil and Natural Gas describes the issues surrounding world oil and natural gas production decline, and their implications for both local economies and the global economic system.

Section 3 Local Challenges, Local Advantages explores why local governments should be concerned about energy and climate uncertainty, and identifies the advantages that local governments have for addressing the problem.

Section 4 Responses to Energy and Climate Uncertainty reviews the experiences of U.S. and Canadian municipalities that have already begun planning for energy and climate uncertainty, and derives "lessons learned" from these actions.

Section 5 Transitioning to the Post Carbon World proposes four initial steps that local governments should take to start addressing energy and climate uncertainty, and five principles to guide long-range planning.

The Appendix includes guidelines for starting a local task force on peak oil, a special section on systems thinking as a tool for municipalities, and other resources.

Who should use this guidebook, and why?

Post Carbon Cities: Planning for Energy and Climate Uncertainty is written specifically for people who work with and for local governments in the U.S. and Canada: elected officials, managers, planners, engineers, policy analysts, program staff and others. Consultants and concerned citizens will also find this guidebook useful for understanding the issues and responsibilities that municipal leaders face in confronting peak oil and global warming.

This guidebook fills a gap in the resources currently available to local government decision-makers on planning for the changing global energy and climate situations of the 21st century. While many resources exist for community energy planning, energy efficiency and greenhouse gas mitigation, little has yet been written for local governments about the challenge of peak oil and the need to begin adapting to those effects of climate change that are now unavoidable.

About the Author

Daniel Lerch is Program Manager of Post Carbon Institute's Post Carbon Cities program. He has worked with urban land use and transportation planning issues for over ten years in the public, private and non-profit sectors, and is a co-founder of The City Repair Project, an award-winning non-profit organization working on community public space issues. Mr. Lerch has a Bachelor of Arts in Urban Studies from Rutgers University in New Jersey and a Master of Urban Studies from Portland State University in Oregon.

Post Carbon Cities program

Post Carbon Cities is a program of Post Carbon Institute. Post Carbon Cities helps local governments understand the challenges posed by peak oil and climate change, and provides resources for elected officials, planners, managers and others to develop plans and responses appropriate to their communities. The Post Carbon Cities website, postcarboncities.net, is a forum for news, discussion, policy tools and other resources related to local government actions on peak oil and global warming. Please visit us online and join this growing movement of cities developing effective local responses to energy and climate uncertainty.

Preface

About Post Carbon Institute

Post Carbon Institute (www.postcarbon.org) helps communities everywhere understand and respond to the challenges of fossil fuel depletion and climate change. We conduct research, develop resources and assist groups and individuals who are leading their communities in making a smooth transition to a world that is no longer dependent on hydrocarbon fuels nor emitting climate-changing levels of carbon: the post-carbon world.

Post Carbon Institute is headquartered in Sebastopol, California with offices in Washington, D.C.; Portland, Oregon; Vancouver, British Columbia; and Queensland in Australia. Our advisors and fellows include some of the world's foremost experts on energy resource depletion and sustainability.

Founder and President
Julian Darley

Executive Director
Celine Rich

Fellows and Advisors

Jason Bradford, *Co-founder, Willits Economic Localization, Willits, California, USA*

Colin Campbell, *Founder, Association for the Study of Peak Oil and Natural Gas, Ballydehob, Ireland*

Julian Darley, *Author,* **High Noon for Natural Gas***, Sebastopol, California, USA*

Richard Douthwaite, *Founder, Foundation for the Economics of Sustainability (FEASTA), Dublin, Ireland*

David Fridley, *Staff Scientist, Lawrence Berkeley National Laboratory, Berkeley, California, USA*

Richard Heinberg, *Author,* **Powerdown** *and* **The Party's Over***, California, USA*

Dave Hughes, *Petroleum Geologist, Geological Survey of Canada, Calgary, Alberta, Canada*

James Kunstler, *Author,* **The Long Emergency** *and* **The Geography of Nowhere***, New York, USA*

Jeremy Leggett, *CEO, Solarcentury, London, UK*

William Rees, *Professor, University of British Columbia, Vancouver, British Columbia, Canada*

Hermann Scheer, *Member of the German Bundestag and President, Eurosolar, Berlin, Germany*

Ed Schreyer, *former Governor General of Canada (1979-1984), Manitoba, Canada*

Acknowledgements

This Guidebook was developed in part through interviews, meetings and reviews with knowledgeable elected officials, planners, architects, scholars and advocates. Many thanks to the following people for lending their valuable insights:

Michael Armstrong
   Operations Manager, Portland Office of Sustainable Development, Portland, Oregon
Richard Balfour
   Principal, Balfour & Associates, Vancouver, British Columbia
Richard Bell
   Communications Director, Post Carbon Institute, Washington, D.C.
Mia Birk
   Principal, Alta Planning + Design, Portland, Oregon
Stephan Brown
   Ph.D. student, Portland State University, Portland, Oregon
Rex Burkholder
   Councilmember, Metro regional government, Portland, Oregon
Colin Campbell
   Founder, Association for the Study of Peak Oil & Gas, Ballydehob, Ireland
Debbie Cook
   Councilmember, Huntington Beach, California
Derek Corrigan
   Mayor, Burnaby, British Columbia

Post Carbon Institute

Brian Corzilius
  Willits Economic Localization, Willits, California
Julian Darley
  President, Post Carbon Institute, Sebastopol, California
Bryn Davidson
  Principal, Rao-D Cityworks, Vancouver, British Columbia
Ed Delhagen
  Deputy Director, Vermont Sustainable Jobs Fund, Montpelier, Vermont
Matt Emlen
  Peak Oil Task Force staff, Portland, Oregon
Alan Falleri
  Directory of Community Development, Willits, California
Brendan Finn
  Chief of Staff, Commissioner Dan Saltzman, Portland, Oregon
Eric Garza
  Ph.D. student, School of Public and Environmental Affairs, Indiana Univ., Bloomington, Indiana
Michael Jordan
  Chief Operating Officer, Metro regional government, Portland, Oregon
James Howard Kunstler
  *Author, **The Long Emergency** and **The Geography of Nowhere**, New York*
Brooke Lerch
  Quality Management Lead Assessor (ret.), Det Norske Veritas, Flemington, New Jersey
Kathy Leotta
  Lead Transportation Planner, Parsons Brinckerhoff, Seattle, Washington
Noelle Mackay
  Executive Director, Vermont Forum on Sprawl, Burlington, Vermont
Larry Menkes
  Chair, Energy Advisory Committee, Warminster Twp., Pennsylvania
Bill McKibben
  *Author, **End of Nature**; Middlebury College Scholar-in-Residence, Middlebury, Vermont*
Anton Nelessen
  Principal, A. Nelessen Associates, Princeton, New Jersey
Ron Orenstein
  Councilmember, Willits, California
Glen Peace
  City Manager, Hamilton, Ontario
Sam Pierce
  Mayor, Sebastopol, California
Frank Popper
  Professor, Rutgers Univ., New Brunswick, New Jersey
Deborah Popper
  Associate Professor, City Univ. of New York, Staten Island, New York
Gordon Price
  Director, City Program, Simon Fraser Univ., Vancouver, British Columbia
Stuart Ramsey
  Transportation Planner, Burnaby, British Columbia
William Rees
  Professor, School of Community & Regional Planning, Univ. of British Columbia, Vancouver, British Columbia
Richard Register
  President, Ecocity Builders, Oakland, California

Preface

Celine Rich
Executive Director, Post Carbon Institute, Sebastopol, California
Steve Robichaud
Manager, Growth Management, Hamilton, Ontario
Larry Robinson
Councilmember, Sebastopol, California
Dave Rollo
Councilmember, Bloomington, Indiana
Leonie Sandercock
Director, School of Community & Regional Planning, Univ. of British Columbia, Vancouver, British Columbia
Scott Sawyer
Vermont Sustainable Jobs Fund, Montpelier, Vermont
Paul Sears
Scientist, Natural Resources Canada, Ottawa, Ontario
John Sechrest
Economic Development Specialist, Corvallis-Benton Chamber Coalition, Corvallis, Oregon
Ethan Seltzer
Director, School of Urban Studies and Planning, Portland State Univ., Portland, Oregon
Chris Skrebowski
Editor, Petroleum Review, London, England
Paul Smith
Manager, Transportation Planning Division, Portland, Oregon
Charlie Stephens
Oregon Department of Energy (ret.), Salem, Oregon
Greg Strong
Spring Hill Solutions, Burlington, Vermont
Dell Tredinnick
Project Development Manager, City of Santa Rosa, California
Cliff Wood
Councilmember, Providence, Rhode Island
...plus many others who have assisted in this project.

And special thanks to:
my mother, for inspiring me to make my work meaningful;
my father, for teaching me to look at the world with a critical eye and a hopeful heart;
and Ariel, for her boundless patience, support and love.

1. Introduction

1.1 **The new challenge of uncertainty** **Over just the last few years, major government, business and community leaders in the United States and Canada have been changing their expectations about the future of energy and the environment.**

Most credible observers now recognize that our global energy supply and our global climate face radical change in the coming decades if we do not radically change the way our industrialized economies consume energy. Global warming is widely accepted as a serious problem needing immediate and far-reaching action. Peak oil—the coming decline of global oil production—is not as widely understood, but presents a similarly complex set of challenges.

The problem posed by peak oil and global warming is ultimately one of *uncertainty*: both phenomena are creating changes in economies and ecosystems at the global, regional and even local levels that we cannot easily predict. For local governments—responsible for managing local public services and planning for future land use and transportation—this new uncertainty creates a wide variety of risks and vulnerabilities. How will local jobs be affected when the price of oil reaches $200 per barrel? How will regional climate shifts affect local water supplies? Local governments need to understand and respond to these challenges.

This section will:

— introduce the issues of peak oil and global warming,

— describe how these phenomena are creating uncertainty about our energy supplies and climate, and

— explain the urgency for local governments to address this pressing problem.

One thing is clear: the era of easy oil is over... [M]any of the world's oil and gas fields are maturing. And new energy discoveries are mainly occurring in places where resources are difficult to extract, physically, economically, and even politically.

– From Chevron's "Will You Join Us?" advertising campaign, February 2006

...[W]e have at most ten years – not ten years to decide upon action, but ten years to alter fundamentally the trajectory of global greenhouse emissions.

– James Hansen, Director, NASA Goddard Institute for Space Studies, "The Threat to the Planet," New York Review of Books, 13 July 2006

Introduction

1.2 Peak oil and energy uncertainty
A changing world

The fundamental factors of world oil supply and demand are changing. Global demand for oil is rising as the less-developed world—led by China and India—rapidly industrializes, and the developed world continues to grow. The giant oil fields of the 20th century are declining, however, and oil discoveries have been declining since the mid-1960s. Major oil companies like Chevron admit that much of the most-easily accessible oil has already been extracted, making oil production increasingly dependent on significant and expensive changes in production methods.[1]

World oil production is also becoming increasingly concentrated in countries at risk of instability and countries that are rivals to Western economic interests; Saudi Arabia, Russia, China, Iran and Venezuela together account for nearly 35% of world production. Oil and natural gas are powerful political tools that producer countries like Russia and Iran have increasingly proven willing to use, or threaten to use, to further their own interests.

The responses to these changes vary widely. Some scientists and advocates focus on an impending peak of world oil production when oil companies will no longer be able to increase production to meet demand. Some political leaders, especially in the U.S., take an "energy security" approach focusing on how foreign oil dependence creates worrisome economic and military vulnerabilities. Still others maintain that there is no near-term problem, and that we can rely on market forces to develop substitutes for oil, better oil production technology, and more oil-efficient products.

Experts may disagree on what these changes mean and how we should respond to them, but it's important to note that nearly everyone agrees on at least two things: fundamental changes in global oil supply and demand are *real* and are happening *now*.

One of the main problems arising from these changes in global oil supply and demand is the potential for higher and more volatile oil prices. As a recent report for the U.S. Department of Energy noted,

> ...a shortfall of oil supplies caused by world conventional oil production peaking will sharply increase oil prices and oil price volatility. As oil peaking is approached, relatively minor events will likely have more pronounced impacts on oil prices and futures markets.[2]

"Oil peaking"—or "peak oil"—refers to the point at which total global oil production cannot grow any further and begins to decline, an event that an increasing number of petroleum analysts predict happening by 2010. Ultimately, knowing the exact date is not critical. What matters is that oil prices will become volatile and progressively higher when demand increases and supply can't keep up.

The ready and cheap supply of oil and natural gas is currently as presupposed and essential to our economy as the supply of potable water is to our communities.

A big problem

None of this would be a real concern if the commodity in question were soybeans or pork bellies: demand and supply would find a new equilibrium without fundamentally threatening the global economy. Oil, however, is unlike any other commodity in three important ways.

First, oil is absolutely essential to the most basic functions of the industrialized world. Oil is the key raw material for gasoline, diesel, jet fuel, home heating oil, industrial oils, many chemicals and most plastics. Many industries are extremely dependent on oil in multiple forms; for example, the modern global food production and distribution system uses oil as a fuel for farming and transporting, and as a raw material for agrichemicals and packaging plastics. Instability in oil supply and price has serious potential consequences for virtually all sectors of the global economy, particularly transportation, agriculture and manufacturing.

Second, there are currently no viable substitutes for oil at current rates of consumption. Oil is unlike any other raw material on earth in its "embodied" energy and practical applications. Although alternatives to oil do exist for many of its uses, whether as a transportable fuel (biofuels, fuel cells) or as a raw material (cellulosic plastics, biopesticides), these are generally vastly inferior to oil as resources for these applications. The logistical difficulty of shifting to oil substitutes is so great that even the European Union, which has pursued alternatives to oil use far more aggressively than the U.S. and Canada, has been able to set only a modest goal of increasing the biofuel share of all its transport fuels to 5.75% by 2010.

Finally, and most importantly, our entire economic system is built on the assumption that oil will always be readily available at affordable prices. The modern world's complex inter-firm and inter-governmental economic relationships, made up of movements of raw materials and goods across the globe, very much depend on the price and availability of oil being relatively predictable. If the price of oil becomes very high or very volatile or both, the globalized economy as a whole will face fundamental challenges.

The threat of global oil supply not meeting demand (whether or not it's referred to as "peak oil") is already creating change and uncertainty in diverse sectors of the global economy—for example, meat prices are rising because corn crops are being diverted to ethanol production[3]. At a broader scale, the threat of serious oil price volatility means our past assumptions about energy supplies and prices no longer hold. Throughout this guidebook, we'll refer to these peak oil-induced uncertainties in the global economy as *"energy uncertainty."*

1.3 **Global warming and climate uncertainty** At the 1992 UN "Earth Summit" in Rio de Janeiro, most of the world's governments agreed that global warming was a real and serious problem for all of humanity. It took fifteen years of politically-charged debate and half-hearted measures, however, before a critical mass of trans-national corporations and Western government, business and media leaders finally accepted the need to take serious and immediate action against greenhouse gas emissions[4].

Although there is agreement that global warming has serious environmental, economic and social ramifications, there is still disagreement on what exactly will happen, when it will happen and what the specific regional and local effects will be. How will global warming shift regional growing seasons and water supplies? How likely is that major climate functions like the Gulf Stream will be fundamentally altered, and what impact will that have on our cities and economies? Is there a tipping point of carbon dioxide levels that, once reached, will trigger "runaway" climate change?[5]

Whereas peak oil and its effects have the potential to set off massive global economic disruption, global warming and its effects have the potential to set off massive global ecological disruption—which will then affect the global economy. Throughout this guidebook, we'll refer to these global warming-induced uncertainties about the environment and the economy as *"climate uncertainty."*

1.4 **A job for government** In the U.S. and Canada, it's generally accepted—at least in theory—that government should play a role where market forces cannot be expected (or trusted) to achieve fair and acceptable results for the common good. We expect our governments to ensure that basic services like utilities, schools and police protection are

Oil (and natural gas) are the essential components in the fertilizer on which world agriculture depends; oil makes it possible to transport food to the totally non-self-sufficient megacities of the world. Oil also provides the plastics and chemicals that are the bricks and mortar of contemporary civilization...

– Daniel Yergin, *The Prize: The Epic Quest for Oil, Money, and Power.* 1991

Introduction

available universally, and not just to the highest bidders. We also expect our governments to safeguard, to some extent, the environment and the economy: we regulate pollution and break up monopolies.

Global warming and peak oil are problems that market forces alone cannot solve in the most desirable ways for the common good. Markets respond to price signals—but mitigating the causes and preparing for the effects of global warming and peak oil takes years of broad, concerted effort. If we wait for price signals to start planning, it will be too late, and our economies and communities (and certainly the environment) will suffer.

Looking at the vulnerabilities created by peak oil and global warming, we must weigh the certain costs of acting against the potential costs of not acting. According to a growing number of analysts in both the public and private sectors, the risks of not addressing these vulnerabilities are economically and socially so great that it is in the interest of society that governments act now.

1.5 A job for municipalities Kathleen Leotta, Lead Transportation Planner with the multinational planning and engineering firm Parsons Brinckerhoff, researches how oil supply disruptions affect transportation systems, and what transportation management strategies have worked best in such scenarios. In studying the effects of Hurricane Katrina in 2005, she found that municipalities as far away as North Carolina were left to fend for themselves after regional pipelines carrying motor fuels were shut down:

A huge amount of their motor fuels was cut off; they didn't seem to quite realize how much of their finished fuels came through the pipelines. The state held the largest stockpiles of fuel, and when all the municipalities came to them to ask if they could give them some of their fuel, they said they couldn't because they didn't have enough for their own vehicles and fleets.

It's really the case that municipalities need to start thinking about some of these things on their own.[6]

Know your municipality's vulnerabilities, because there isn't necessarily anyone else thinking about them.

Natural disasters are unusual and extreme events, but this story nevertheless has a valuable lesson for local government leaders: Know your municipality's vulnerabilities, because there isn't necessarily anyone else thinking about them.

Identifying and mitigating community vulnerabilities is one of the more important—if often unwritten—expectations we have of our local governments. Unfortunately, as with many other undertakings that aren't immediate or regular priorities, local governments often don't have the resources to address such vulnerabilities except in times of crisis, when it's too late to prepare.

Preparing for energy and climate uncertainty is much different than preparing for a hurricane, of course. In 2006, many municipalities saw first-hand how spikes in global oil prices directly and immediately impacted their core responsibilities when quickly rising asphalt prices caused street maintenance costs in many municipalities to double or even triple

Identifying and mitigating community vulnerabilities is probably one of the more important—if often unwritten—expectations we have of our local governments.

over 2005 (see *Box 5*, page 26). Changes in a fundamental economic factor like the price of oil—or a fundamental environmental factor like average temperatures—can have unexpected system effects that are difficult to predict.

Oil and energy prices affect just about everything a local governments can do, from providing basic services like public works and emergency response to long-range land use and transportation planning. The local effects of climate change are more difficult to predict, but they generally threaten many of the basic "ecological goods and services" that cities depend on, such as water supplies and favorable agricultural conditions. Prudent governments will want to identify their local vulnerabilities as early as possible and address them carefully and comprehensively.

1.6 **Planning for energy and climate uncertainty** We haven't really needed to think about fundamental energy issues since the oil crises of the 1970s because the global system of oil production and distribution has largely ensured the availability of oil at relatively affordable prices. As a municipal leader, this has meant that you could do everything you needed to do—from updating the annual operating budget to getting multi-million dollar transportation projects into the federal funding process—without needing to consider the price or availability of energy in your community as a significant variable.

> ## The challenge for municipalities is not to predict the future, but to approach the future with the right tools and the right information.

How, then, do we plan municipal budgets and activities when nobody knows if the price of oil will steadily increase by 100% over the next five years, or spike next month for just a week, or stay right where it is for a decade? How do we plan for the local effects of climate change when they could very well range from relatively manageable to catastrophic? Any particular ten-year scenario of energy and climate trends will have unique implications for municipal responsibilities, and planning for the wrong scenario could end up being much more expensive than not planning at all.

As we'll explore throughout this Guidebook, the challenge for municipalities is not to predict the future, but to approach the future with the right tools and the right information. While most municipalities share some basic oil and gas vulnerabilities—such as in fuel for operating city vehicles and heating city buildings—the exact response that any one municipality undertakes will be unique because the context within which each municipality operates is unique. For this reason, we've focused the body of the Guidebook on general issues and process guidelines, instead of suggesting a one-size-fits-all response program or risk assessment template.

1.7 **Urgency to act** Time is short to prepare for peak oil and global warming. At current rates of fossil fuel consumption we will likely pass the peak of global oil production by 2010 (some analysts believe we have passed it already), and we seriously risk triggering catastrophic climate change if we do not start significantly reducing carbon emissions in the next ten years[7]. Local governments around the world need to act quickly and decisively.

Planetizen.com, the largest online network of city planners in the United States, named "Peak Oil and Planning for Alternative Energy" one of the Top Ten Planning Issues of 2005. It's important for municipalities to address both peak oil and global warming, not only to prepare their communities for an uncertain future but also to stay competitive with other municipalities and regions competing for firms and households. Those communities that manage these challenges successfully will have an advantage over those that don't.

Dealing with local dependencies on oil and natural gas—two of the most important materials to modern society, and simultaneously the most damaging to the climate—can be an extremely challenging and at times overwhelming task for local government leaders, both as public servants and as private citizens. Local communities can be extremely resilient, however, and time and again prove they are able to manage disruptive change. It's our hope that this Guidebook will help your community navigate these challenges as smoothly as possible.

2. The End of Cheap Oil and Natural Gas

Some petroleum geologists have said that a peak in world oil production followed by steady decline is inevitable and coming soon. Some authors have said that modern economies could collapse for a want of energy after peak oil. Some economists have said that high oil prices will simply encourage the global market to produce cheaper substitutes. Still others (albeit far fewer) have said that there is plenty of oil around to meet global needs through most of the 21st Century. Who is right?

In a way, all of them are:

- Many respected petroleum geologists agree that global oil production will peak within the next ten years (and some think it may have peaked already), followed by a permanent decline.

- The modern industrial world could in fact face extremely serious challenges following a peak—including consistently rising prices, sudden price spikes, and even shortages—if it is not managed well.

- High oil and natural gas prices have made more expensive oil sources profitable to exploit, and alternative energy technologies like solar, wind and biofuel have seen a surge of entrepreneurial investment in recent years.

And finally:

- Theoretically there may be enough oil in alternate forms like tar sands and coal (via a process called "liquefaction") to meet the needs of a growing industrial world for some time. However, the energy costs, technological costs, environmental costs and political machinations that would be needed to produce this oil at large scale make this unlikely and generally undesirable.

Peak oil is a contentious issue because its implications are enormous, touching everything from the way we live our daily lives to the way we run the largest of corporations and nations. New England author and scholar Bill McKibben has compared the "end of the oil age," together with global warming, to a vise grip squeezing the modern world, observing that we face "very significant, very big changes in a very short amount of time."

The oil market will remain fairly stable in the very near term, but with steadily increasing prices as world production approaches its peak. The doubling of oil prices from 2003-2005 is not an anomaly, but a picture of the future. Oil production is approaching its peak; low growth in availability can be expected for the next 5 to 10 years. As worldwide petroleum production peaks, geopolitics and market economics will cause even more significant price increases and security risks.

One can only speculate at the outcome from this scenario as world petroleum production declines. The disruption of world oil markets may also affect world natural gas markets since most of the natural gas reserves are co-located with the oil reserves.

– Donald Fournier and Eileen Westervelt, US Army Corps of Engineers, "Energy Trends and Their Implications for U.S. Army Installations," Sept. 2005

The End of Cheap Oil and Gas

Could a mere 4 percent shortfall in daily oil supply propel the price of a barrel to more than $120 in a matter of days? That's what some oil market experts are saying, and if they're correct, we face the very real possibility of an oil shock wave that could send our economy reeling. Such a rapid rise in fuel costs would have profound effects that could severely threaten the foundation of America's economic prosperity.

- Frederick Smith, CEO of FedEx Corp. and General P. X. Kelley, (ret.), former Reagan Chief of Staff, "Are we ready for the next oil shock?" *The Washington Post*, 11 Aug. 2006

President Bush says we're addicted to oil; we're also addicted to nitrogen fertilizer.

- Marcus Simantel, retired farmer, Portland Peak Oil Task Force

Local governments need to tread carefully on contentious issues, of course, and for good reason. As stewards of public resources, government leaders need to have solid, defensible reasoning behind the policies and programs they pursue.

With this need for a solid foundation in mind, this Section will:

—review the basics of peak oil and peak natural gas,

—explain why the real problem is price volatility,

—discuss why existing alternatives for oil and natural gas are unlikely to substitute fully for oil and natural gas, and

—explore the implications of this complex problem.

2.1 **Uses of oil and natural gas** Oil and natural gas are two of the most valuable materials in the industrialized world. They are used to fuel vehicles and industrial machinery, generate electricity, heat buildings, and manufacture a broad array of products like plastics, fertilizers and industrial chemicals. Many of the most significant developments in the modern world, including the mass production of automobiles, the affordability of inter-continental transport, and the "green revolution" that boosted world agricultural outputs in the 1960s and 1970s, were made possible largely—if not entirely—by affordable oil and gas.

Oil and natural gas are often found together in an oil deposit, although natural gas is also found in its own deposits. Oil is processed chiefly to produce various kinds of liquid fuel, and natural gas is processed chiefly to be delivered as gaseous fuel. Both are also processed to produce various petrochemicals, products of which include plastics, fertilizers, pesticides, solvents, soaps, drugs, explosives, synthetic fibers, paints, and epoxies. Natural gas is also a major source of ammonia (for fertilizers) and hydrogen.

Above all, oil and natural gas are prized for their high energy content. In 2004, these two fuels together provided over half of the non-electricity energy consumed in the United States and Canada in nearly every sector: 53% in the U.S. industrial sector, 76% in the Canadian agricultural sector, and a full 99% in both countries' transportation sectors (see Figure 1). Over 60% of all homes in both the U.S. and Canada are heated with either natural gas or oil.

"Petroleum" is simply a different term for crude oil. Natural gas as delivered to consumers is primarily methane, but when first extracted it may contain other materials such as ethane, propane and butane.

Oil and natural gas together generate a fifth of U.S. electricity. The mix of fuels used for electricity production varies widely across the continent, however, even within regions. For example, Florida produces over half its electricity from petroleum and natural gas, but neighboring Georgia is almost completely reliant on coal and nuclear power. Oil and gas produce under a tenth of Canadian electricity, most of this being natural gas generation in the gas-rich provinces of Alberta and Saskatchewan.

Figure 1:
Energy Sources and Uses (Except Electricity Generation): United States & Canada (2004)

UNITED STATES

Sources	Uses				
	Industry	Transport	Residential	Commercial	Agriculture
Oil	12%	97%	12%	9%	96%
Gas	40%	2%	43%	36%	–
Coal	10%	–	–	1%	3%
Electricity	27%	1%	42%	53%	–
Other	11%	–	4%	1%	–
TOTAL	100%	100%	100%	100%	100%

In the United States, oil and natural gas accounted for over 50% of non-electricity energy use in all but one sector (commercial), 96% of energy use in agriculture, and nearly all energy use in transportation.

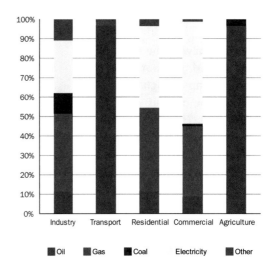

CANADA

Sources	Uses				
	Industry	Transport	Residential	Commercial	Agriculture
Oil	11%	93%	9%	27%	63%
Gas	36%	6%	44%	36%	13%
Coal	6%	–	–	–	–
Electricity	31%	1%	41%	37%	24%
Other	16%	–	6%	–	–
TOTAL	100%	100%	100%	100%	100%

Compared to the United States, Canada depends somewhat less on oil and natural gas for non-electricity energy use in industry and agriculture, but more in the commercial sector. Transportation in Canada is nearly entirely dependent on oil and natural gas.

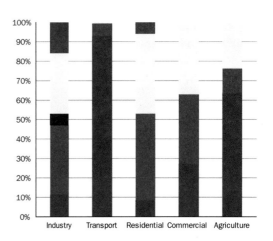

Notes: Data compiled from International Energy Agency "Energy Balance" country statistics, available at http://www.iea.org/Textbase/stats. Percentages derived from consumption data in thousand tonnes of oil equivalent (ktoe) on a net calorific value basis; totals may not add exactly due to rounding. "Other" includes geothermal, solar, wind, tidal, biomass and combustible waste. Data do not account for energy consumption by electricity plants, which includes additional use of oil, natural gas and coal as well as nuclear power and hydropower.

2.2 **Oil supply and demand** There are five big problems with relying on oil as our dominant source of energy and as a key raw material:

1. Oil is a product of geological processes which ended around 85 million years ago, so there's only a **finite amount** of it on the planet.

2. Oil is scattered around the world in underground locations of varying size and accessibility, so while we have pretty good estimates, we **don't truly know how much oil there actually is** until we've extracted it.

3. There's a **time lag for oil to reach the global market**—generally well over three years—after an oil source has been discovered. Plus, the more technologically challenging an oil source is to exploit, the longer it can take to bring it to production. The largest projects, and offshore projects in particular, are now taking six to nine years from discovery to regular oil delivery.[8]

The End of Cheap Oil and Gas

There will always be more oil in the ground, just not enough at a cheap enough price to sustain the current world oil demand... The all-important question is, how much oil can the industry pump every day (that is, at what rate can that oil be produced)? That's what the debate over Peak Oil is all about—not reserves or amounts ultimately recoverable, but flow rates. When will the flow rate that the industry can possibly attain reach its maximum?

– Richard Heinberg (author, *Powerdown*), "Open Letter to Greg Palast", 6 July 2006

The reduced level of spare [oil] production capacity [to under 1.3 million barrels per day] significantly increases the risk to oil prices from a disruption to supply because as many as 20 different countries currently produce at least 1 million barrels per day, including countries such as Iran, Iraq, Nigeria, and Venezuela.

–Energy Information Administration, United States. "STEO Supplement: Why are oil prices so high?" Short Term Energy Outlook, August 2006

4. Nearly half the global oil supply comes from around 120 "giant" oilfields (at least half of which are already in decline[9]) in different parts of the world, each with its own set of technological, environmental and political **factors that can disrupt the flow of oil.**

5. The **price of oil depends on the flow of oil** from fields and reserves to the global market, which in turn depends on OPEC[10] policies, geopolitical events and other factors. OPEC member states limited their oil production for years in order to keep the price of oil from dropping too low. Throughout much of 2005 and 2006, all OPEC producers (except possibly Saudi Arabia) appear to have produced at full capacity in order to keep the price of oil from rising too high.

These five points together form the basis for why more and more people are concerned about a coming "peak" and subsequent decline in world oil production. Let's dig a little deeper into the economics and geology behind these concerns.

Oil flow: the real issue

The price of oil today reflects the market's confidence that an expected amount of oil will be flowing to consumers tomorrow. The business world greets announcements of new oil discoveries with enthusiasm, but if the flow of oil is constrained by obstacles in extraction, refining, or transport, market prices will increase no matter how much oil is thought to be in the ground.

Three main factors determine the *flow* of global oil: the supply of oil available to be delivered, the demand for that supply, and the ability of suppliers to deliver the product to meet demand.

- **Supply:** The global supply of oil available for delivery includes oil in active production, the "spare" production capacity that OPEC (largely Saudi Arabia) maintains as a buffer to produce extra oil when needed, and oil stockpiles held by oil companies, governments and public-private agencies.

  In the short term, the 90-day stockpiles held by most OECD[11] countries and coordinated by the International Energy Agency serve to keep the price of oil stable in times of brief supply disruption, such as after Hurricane Katrina.

  In the medium term, spare production capacity serves as a buffer against supply flow disruptions while new capacity is developed and brought online. OPEC's spare capacity has fallen significantly in recent years, from over 7 million barrels per day in 2002 to under 2 million barrels per day in 2006 and 2007[12].

  In the long term, the total amount of oil in active production across the globe is largely determined by past investments in exploration and technology.

- **Demand**: The global demand of oil per country is generally driven by economic activity, population and level of industrialization. The countries of the western world have long dominated global oil demand, but with the global economic restructuring of the last few decades, oil consumption has increased very quickly in the less-developed world. Chinese demand for oil has grown at a faster annual rate than U.S. demand since the mid-1990s. The U.S. Energy Information Administration projects that, for 2006, China will have been responsible for 38 percent of the increase in demand for oil, a trend that is not expected to change in the foreseeable future.

- **Delivery**: Delivering crude oil from field to consumer requires pumping, refining, and transporting. Any of these steps is liable to disruption by civil unrest, technical problems, forces of nature, or just a lack of infrastructure or operating resources. When regional oil production was interrupted by Hurricanes Katrina and Rita in the Gulf of Mexico in 2005, and then by an armed uprising in Nigeria in 2006, the price of oil increased worldwide. Oil delivery can also be threatened by political events. Facing potential sanctions for continued pursuit of its nuclear program, Iran in June 2006 warned that "if the country's interests are attacked, we will use all our capabilities and oil is one of them." With roughly half of global oil production taking place in countries that aren't necessarily aligned with Western interests—such as Saudi Arabia, Russia,

Iran, China and Venezuela—the potential for politically-motivated disruption will only grow.

The *flow*—and therefore the price—of oil faces pressures in all three of these areas: inflexible and diminishing supply, steadily growing demand, and increasing potential for delivery disruption. Growing demand and the potential for disruption are fairly straightforward issues, so let's take a closer look at the more complicated of these factors: supply, or more specifically, production of that supply.

Oil production: the realities of long term decline

Oil production in a region—a country like Saudi Arabia, or a geographical area like the North Sea—when graphed over time roughly follows a bell curve (see Figure 2, below). The easily-found fields (which also tend to be the largest) go into production first, and cumulative production increases as more fields are added and fields reach their maximum flow rates. As resources allow and as the market demands, more technically-challenging fields are also found and contribute to production. Over time the "easy" fields have all been discovered, and remaining discoveries (usually smaller) depend on challenging and expensive exploration methods.

Generally it takes well over three years for a newly-discovered oil field to begin sending oil to the global market; the delay on large fields can be twice as long. A persistent decline in discoveries therefore means that actual production of oil will inevitably reach a peak and then decline. Later technological advances may uncover previously unknown fields after a region has peaked, adding to cumulative discoveries. However, by the time a region is in its declining phase it has generally been explored so thoroughly that consistent discovery of new large fields is highly unlikely. Also, older fields usually deliver progressively less oil year after year, further contributing to the declining production of a region.

World discoveries of oil peaked in the mid-1960s and have generally declined since, from an average of around 55 billion barrels per year 1960-1965 to an average of under 10 billion barrels per year 2000-2005. Much of the oil we use today comes from the giant Middle East oil fields discovered in the mid-20th century, oil fields that many now suspect are in decline.

Figure 2: Hubbert Curve (conceptual)

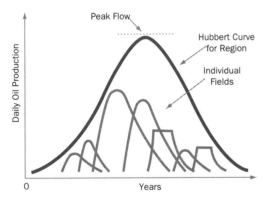

The "Hubbert Curve" describes how the cumulative oil production of a region roughly follows a bell curve. Larger oil deposits tend to be discovered and produced first, producing a "peak" in regional production followed by decline as smaller wells are unable to maintain cumulative production growth. The curve is named after M. King Hubbert, who established the concept while a geophysicist at Shell from 1943 to 1964.

Thus we are producing today what we discovered in the past, while we are discovering little today for the future; in fact, production has generally outpaced discoveries since 1981. In 2005, new yearly discoveries totaled under 9 billion barrels, while consumption was over 31 billion barrels per year; in other words, we consumed 344% more oil than we discovered[13].

Some new oil fields (including potentially large finds such as a six-mile deep Gulf of Mexico reservoir announced by Chevron in September 2006) will continue to be discovered and produced as higher oil prices make more expensive technologies practical. But given the difficulty in locating remaining major fields, plus the enormous expense to produce them, none but the most aggressively optimistic analysts think that a global peak in oil production can be delayed for more than a decade or so. Moreover, the increasing reliance on "non-conventional" oil like tar sands

Christophe de Margerie, head of exploration at [Total,] the French oil giant...says the oil is there...but the amount you can deliver today depends on how many wells you can drill and how fast you can deplete an oilfield, not to mention gaining the co-operation of governments, which guard access to the precious resource jealously. There is no prospect of reaching the lofty peaks that economists at the International Energy Agency predict will be needed to satisfy world demand for oil.

There are not enough engineers, rigs, pipelines and drillers to increase current world output of 85 million barrels per day to 120 million, he says.

– Carl Mortished, "Oilman with a Total solution," The Times (UK). 8 April 2006

The End of Cheap Oil and Gas

and deep-sea oil to prop up global supplies[14] suggests that conventional oil sources are dwindling, as the oil industry is forced to turn to less profitable sources.

Unfortunately, we won't really know if we've passed peak production until it's a few years in the past. We're not certain if the big Saudi oil fields are already in decline because Saudi Arabia's true oil reserve figures are state secrets. The "proved reserves" figures regularly quoted by energy analysts are really only estimates of what's theoretically recoverable based on geological data and current economic conditions. Even official data from oil companies and Western countries are open to interpretation, and subject to misrepresentation[15]. Current and historical production data are readily available through the International Energy Agency (http://www.iea.org/) and federal government agencies; discovery and true reserves data, however, are not. Therefore, to predict the future of world oil production we must look to the conclusions of the geologists, engineers, analysts and investors who make it their business to understand and interpret the global oil system (see Table 1, below).

Predicting the exact year of peak oil is difficult: as oil supplies tighten, prices will rise and demand may be depressed. However, the fundamental long-term supply and demand factors driving peak oil will not easily change. According to an increasing number of petroleum analysts, we seem to be facing an undulating plateau of world oil production from 2007 onward, with permanent decline likely underway by 2010.

Table 1:
Projections of World Oil Production Peaking

Projected Date	Source	Background
2005-2006	Deffeyes, K.S.	Professor Emeritus of Petroleum Geology, Princeton
2006-2007	Bakhtiari, A.M.S.	Iranian oil executive
Bumpy plateau from 2007	Laherrère, J.	Oil company geologist (ret.)*
2007-2009	Simmons, M.R.	Energy investment banker
2008-2018	Aleklett, K.	Assoc. for the Study of Peak Oil[†]
Before 2010	Goodstein, D.	Vice Provost, Cal Tech
No later than 2010	Skrebowski, C.	Editor, *UK Petroleum Review*[‡]
Around 2010	Campbell, C.J.	Oil company geologist (ret.)
After 2010	World Energy Council	Non-governmental org.
2018-2025	Rodgers, M.	Partner, PFC Energy[§]
After 2020	CERA	Energy consultants
2025 or later	Shell	Major oil company
2037	US EIA avg.scenario	USGS and USDoE
No visible peak	Lynch, M.C.	Energy economist

Adapted from Hirsch, R. et al. "Peaking of World Oil Production: Impacts, Mitigation, and Risk Management". Report for the U.S. Department of Energy, February 2005.

* Laherrère, J., Communication with Post Carbon Institute, 14 August 2007.

† Aleklett, K., "Global warming exaggerated, insufficient oil, natural gas and coal." *Dagens Nyheter,* 18 May 2007.

‡ Skrebowski, C., Communication with Post Carbon Institute, 14 August 2007.

§ From Kerr, R. A. "Bumpy Road Ahead for World's Oil." *Science,* 18 November 2005. 310:5751, pp.1106-110.

Box 1   Mixed views on the future of oil

Even experts in the oil business are uncertain about the future of oil.

The U.S. Energy Information Administration annually publishes projections for global oil production and prices. As the excerpt at top shows, possible scenarios range widely; they have also changed considerably over previous years. At bottom, recent advertisements by Chevron and ExxonMobil show disagreement about the future of the world's oil supplies.

Oil Price Cases Show Uncertainty in Prospects for World Oil Markets

Figure 29. World oil prices in three cases, 1980-2030 (2004 dollars per barrel)

World oil price projections in the *AEO2006* reference case, in terms of the average price of imported low-sulfur crude oil to U.S. refiners, are considerably higher than those presented in the *AEO2005* reference case. The higher price path in the reference case does not result from different assumptions about the ultimate size of world oil resources but rather anticipates a lower level of future investment in production capacity in key resource-rich regions and a reassessment of the willingness of OPEC to produce at higher rates than projected in last year's outlook.

The historical record shows substantial variability in world oil prices, and there is arguably even more uncertainty about future prices in the long term. *AEO2006* considers three price cases, allowing an assessment of alternative views on the course of future oil prices (Figure 29). In the reference case, world oil prices moderate from current levels to $47 per barrel in 2014, before rising to $57 per barrel in 2030 (2004 dollars). The low and high price cases define a wide range of potential world oil price paths, which in 2030 range from $34 to $96 per barrel. This variability is meant to show the uncertainty about prospects for future world oil resources and economics.

U.S. Energy Information Administration, Annual Energy Overview 2006, p. 64

Chevron advertisement, 2006

ExxonMobil advertisement, 2006

The End of Cheap Oil and Gas

2.3 **Natural gas supply and demand** The problems we face with natural gas are largely the same as the problems we face with oil: global discoveries peaked decades ago, global demand is growing, and its delivery is vulnerable to disruption.

In addition, natural gas is much harder to transport than oil, with only two real choices: as a gas via a network of pipelines, or as a super-cooled liquid ("liquefied natural gas," or LNG) via special transport ships and transfer terminals. Most natural gas used in North America comes via pipeline from fields in Alberta, Alaska, Texas and the Gulf of Mexico. Canada is a net exporter of natural gas, whereas the U.S. imports over 16% of its natural gas, mostly via pipeline from Western Canada. Both the U.S. and Canada are trying to build more LNG import terminals, albeit against increasing local community resistance on security and environmental grounds.

North American discoveries of natural gas peaked in 1960; natural gas production in North America likely peaked early in this decade and is already in long-term decline[16]. Although production is rising in the Rocky Mountains, and new production may commence

in the Arctic (after many years and tens of billions of dollars in investment), these reserves are the last gasp of the continent's gas. North America accounts for almost 30% of world gas extraction, but only has 4% of the reserves.

Further complicating the situation is the trend of natural gas production and consumption in the world's other big gas consumer, Europe. The European Union and Norway together have barely 3% of the world gas reserve, and the biggest producer, Britain, peaked in both oil and gas around the turn of the millennium. With the exception of the very difficult Arctic Barents Sea region, European gas (and oil) discovery has been minimal in recent years, and geological trend analysis suggests that there is little more to find. At current rates of production and with no more discoveries, the EU and Norway will stop producing gas within 30 years. The EU already imports 60% of its gas.

These trends mean that the United States, Europe and Canada are increasingly dependent on imports of natural gas to meet domestic demand. Unfortunately, this is happening at a time when many countries in the developing world—including other natural gas producers like Russia, Iran, Venezuela and Turkmenistan—are also expanding their demand for gas. The vast pipeline network and the complex LNG system is tying diverse consuming nations ever more closely together, so that high prices in North America or Britain will drive up the price of gas for everyone and increase both price and supply volatility.

2.4 **Unconventional oil and substitutes** As oil and natural gas supplies diminish, governments and corporations will search for materials and technologies to replace these resources in their various applications.

Oil and natural gas have advantages as fuels that limit the ways in which other fuels may substitute for them:

- Oil is extremely valuable in part because it is easily transportable as a raw material, and can be refined into a high-energy transportable liquid fuel, such as gasoline or diesel, for easy distribution and use in vehicles.

- Natural gas is a relatively environmentally friendly hydrocarbon fuel, releasing the lowest amount of greenhouse gases per unit of all the fossil fuels; its primarily fuel uses are heat, motors and electricity generation.[17]

Both oil and natural gas have a high energy return on investment (EROI)[18] for their fuel uses, when compared to substitute fuels. For example, US conventional oil (with an energy content of 138,000 btu per gallon) has an EROI ratio of over 20, whereas biofuel ethanol (with an energy content of 75,700 btu per gallon) has an EROI ratio of under 2.[19]

The replacement of oil and natural gas in their non-fuel capacities is more complex. Both are raw materials for many different kinds of chemical and plastic products, and natural gas is a key raw material for production of agricultural fertilizer and hydrogen.

With these characteristics in mind, let's take a look at the most commonly-considered substitutes for conventional oil and natural gas:

- **Deepwater and polar oil**

    These terms refer to deposits that are especially difficult to discover and produce because they are located in areas of great ocean depth or in arctic locations choked with ice. Recent technological advances spurred by the rising price of oil are making deepwater oil more profitable: in September 2006, Chevron Corp. announced a successful test drill of an unusually large deepwater deposit in the Gulf of Mexico. Also, global warming is opening up arctic areas that were previously unreachable, spurring oil exploration plans for those regions. These sources will always be inherently riskier and more expensive than the relatively "easy" near-surface old reservoirs of Texas and Saudi Arabia.

- **Tar sands and oil shale**

    Tar sands and oil shale yield substitutes for conventional oil when refined and upgraded. Tar sand is low-quality oil that has migrated to a shallow depth, and is found as a mixture of clay, sand, water and bitumen (a heavy oil). The world's main tar sand fields are in Alberta and Venezuela. Oil shale is immature oil source rock that was not heated enough to become regular oil; the largest oil shale deposits are in the border area between Colorado, Utah and Wyoming. The refining of both materials into useable oil is fraught with many technological challenges, not the least of which is the volume of material that needs to be excavated—and the amount of energy used to heat and otherwise process it—to produce usable oil, roughly two tons of tar sand per barrel of oil equivalent.[20]

    Of special concern is the current use of natural gas to heat tar sands in the refining process; as natural gas supplies tighten and prices become more volatile, tar sand production may quickly become financially infeasible. Finally, the entire production and refinement process of these materials as currently practiced is considerably damaging to the environment as it involves massive scales of strip mining, water pollution, and greenhouse gas emissions.

- **Coal**

    Coal is a major fuel for generating electricity and producing steel, particularly in the U.S. and China. It is also a potential substitute for oil as a *liquid* fuel via the "coal liquefaction" process used successfully in Germany and Japan during World War II. While coal is generally thought to be the most plentiful fossil fuel on earth, a 2007 analysis of recent massive revisions in national coal reserves data found that global coal production could actually peak in as little as 15 years.[21]

    Coal has proven environmentally disastrous as an energy source, from its strip mining to the release of greenhouse gases and toxins in its burning. While technological advances have made it possible to reduce emissions of some pollutants (such as sulfur, nitrogen and mercury) with smokestack "scrubbers," there are significant economic and political barriers to these solutions being universally adopted on both new and existing plants around the world any time soon.

    Advocates of even more massive use of coal talk of designing coal-fired power plants in which carbon dioxide will be captured and "sequestered" (pumped underground) to mitigate global warming. However, this technology is still relatively new and has not yet been applied to working coal-fired power plants.[22]

The massive machinery used to excavate and transport tar sands in Alberta dwarfs a conventional bulldozer.

The End of Cheap Oil and Gas

- **Nuclear**

Nuclear power is used to generate electricity, and so cannot substitute for oil and gas in their capacities as transportable fuels (i.e., for non-electric motor vehicles). Nuclear technology has improved in safety over the years, and nuclear power has attracted some interest as a supposedly "greenhouse gas free" energy source.

However, nuclear power still faces enormous economic, environmental, political and even fuel source challenges:

- Nuclear power plants are still extremely expensive to construct and decommission. Although the nuclear industry claims to have significantly cut investment costs with its new generation of power plant designs, recent analyses by both the U.S. Department of Energy and Standard and Poor's recognize the continuing probability of significant cost overruns.[23]

- Nuclear industry mishaps—from public financing debacles like Shoreham (Long Island, New York) and WPPSS (Washington Public Power Supply System) to accidents like Three Mile Island and Chernobyl—are reminders of the potentially disastrous financial, ecological and public health risks nuclear power still presents.

- Uranium is a limited resource, and there is concern that global uranium demand could exceed supply in a matter of decades if nuclear power is pursued vigorously.[24]

- The nuclear industry has yet to develop a reliable method for storing nuclear waste for the hundreds of thousands of years it would remain dangerously radioactive.

And of greatest concern is the tight coupling between nuclear power programs and the proliferation of nuclear weapons. The international regime that was established to regulate the spread of nuclear power has failed to control the concurrent proliferation of nuclear weapons, as we have seen in North Korea and Iran.

- **Hydrogen**

Hydrogen has made some advances in the last decade as an electricity producer via fuel cells, but fuel cell technology remains expensive, keeping hydrogen marginal as a contributor to overall energy use. The chief problem with hydrogen, however, is that it must be produced from some other material—such as natural gas—making it an energy carrier instead of a true energy source.

Hydrogen is generally produced from natural gas, which has its own problems of supply and price; and with current technology, hydrogen is still quite expensive to produce. Also, hydrogen gas presents a number of logistical challenges, including its low volumetric energy, its extreme flammability, and the lack of widespread infrastructure for its distribution and use. While there are suggestions that these hurdles may be overcome in time, hydrogen is not technically feasible as a mass-production fuel for the near future.

- **Biological**

Ethanol, biodiesel and other biofuels have received increasing attention as "clean," domestically-produced replacements for gasoline and diesel. There are serious challenges to producing biofuels at industrial scales, however, particularly with regard to the amount of energy needed for their cultivation, processing and long-distance transport. Also, increased biofuel crop cultivation is already impacting world food prices, as many farmers replace food crops with more valuable biofuel crops.[25]

Biofuels hold more promise as small-scale, less capital-intensive localized energy sources, where locally-grown crops can be processed into fuel for local use. Organic pesticides and fertilizers exist as substitutes for agrichemicals produced from oil and natural gas; their use has increased in recent years thanks in part to growing interest in organic food and growing concern about pest resistance, water contamination, and worker exposure.

- **Renewables (Hydroelectric, Wind, Solar, Geothermal)**

  Modern hydropower and wind power technologies are used primarily to generate electricity, and thus have limited substitutability for oil and gas as fuels for heating and transportation (at least for the existing fleet of vehicles) in North America. Solar power has long been captured for heat, and more recently, geothermal technology (including ground source heat pumps) has been used to heat and cool buildings. Solar and geothermal power are also both used worldwide to generate electricity.

  Wind and solar technologies have improved greatly since the 1970s, and newer technologies such as tide and wave turbines have promise as well. Hydropower, however, has limited prospects for expansion as many practical locations for large-scale projects have already been developed, and new projects face increasing environmental challenges. Other than hydropower, renewables are still relatively marginal at national levels as power sources but have recently received significant new investment, especially for decentralized applications. According to the United Nations Environment Program, investment in renewable energy worldwide grew from $27.5 billion in 2004 to $49.6 billion in 2005, and then to $70.9 billion in 2006, a total increase of 158%.

2.5 **The implications** If oil and natural gas—two of the most valuable substances for running the modern industrial world—are soon facing permanent decline, and there are no easy ways to substitute for these materials, what are the implications?

Oil and gas price volatility

If global supply clearly becomes unable to meet global demand, a whole host of economic responses, political responses and dynamic interactions would start to occur that are too complex to reasonably predict. All we know is that the conditions described in the sections above create an increasing likelihood of price rise and price *volatility*.

Oil and gas price volatility simply means that the price (ultimately, the *supply*) of these materials is subject to unpredictable and sometimes significant change. We have already seen examples of unusual oil price volatility in the last few years: at the New York Mercantile Exchange (NYMEX) between mid-2004 and mid-2006, "light sweet" crude oil jumped over 20% in five different three-month periods, and similarly dropped more than 15% in four different three-month periods. Faced with such price swings, it becomes harder for governments, businesses and households to budget for the costs of oil and gas products.

Won't the global economy respond?

What does peak oil mean over the long run? "Doomsayers" on one side warn of imminent mass shortages and the ensuing collapse of the global economic system. "Cornucopians" on the other side say not to worry, because corporations and investors will automatically respond to higher oil prices with investments in exploration and technologies, quickly bringing supplies up and prices down.

Both extremes are probably wrong and, interestingly, for the same reason: they misunderstand the *system rigidity* of the global political-economic system as it relates to oil. "System rigidity" means that a system tries to maintain its structure and functioning in the face of immediate changes; but while this contributes to system survival, too much rigidity may keep the system from adapting to changes.

In a system like the global economy, system rigidity means that major global businesses and governments will labor mightily to deal with short term threats to the flow of oil relatively quickly. But it also means that serious preparation for longer-term changes in oil supplies may not receive more attention until disruptions are more frequent and severe. Market responses are largely price-driven, but because new investments take years to bring oil to the market, there will necessarily be a time lag between new price signals and new oil flow.

During this time lag, existing supply will not be able to meet demand, causing prices to rise and both demand and economic activity to fall. These interim

Box 2   The U.S. Department of Energy "Hirsch Report" on peak oil

Excerpted from "Peaking of World Oil Production: Impacts, Mitigation, & Risk Management," prepared by Robert Hirsch et al. for the U.S. Department of Energy, February 2005:

The peaking of world oil production presents the U.S. and the world with an unprecedented risk management problem. As peaking is approached, liquid fuel prices and price volatility will increase dramatically, and, without timely mitigation, the economic, social, and political costs will be unprecedented. Viable mitigation options exist on both the supply and demand sides, but to have substantial impact, they must be initiated more than a decade in advance of peaking...

Important observations and conclusions from this study are as follows:

1. When world oil peaking will occur is not known with certainty. A fundamental problem in predicting oil peaking is the poor quality of and possible political biases in world oil reserves data. Some experts believe peaking may occur soon. This study indicates that "soon" is within 20 years.

2. The problems associated with world oil production peaking will not be temporary, and past "energy crisis" experience will provide relatively little guidance. The challenge of oil peaking deserves immediate, serious attention, if risks are to be fully understood and mitigation begun on a timely basis.

3. Oil peaking will create a severe liquid fuels problem for the transportation sector, not an "energy crisis" in the usual sense that term has been used.

4. Peaking will result in dramatically higher oil prices, which will cause protracted economic hardship in the United States and the world. However, the problems are not insoluble. Timely, aggressive mitigation initiatives addressing both the supply and the demand sides of the issue will be required.

5. In the developed nations, the problems will be especially serious. In the developing nations peaking problems have the potential to be much worse.

6. Mitigation will require a minimum of a decade of intense, expensive effort, because the scale of liquid fuels mitigation is inherently extremely large.

7. While greater end-use efficiency is essential, increased efficiency alone will be neither sufficient nor timely enough to solve the problem. Production of large amounts of substitute liquid fuels will be required. A number of commercial or near-commercial substitute fuel production technologies are currently available for deployment, so the production of vast amounts of substitute liquid fuels is feasible with existing technology.

8. Intervention by governments will be required, because the economic and social implications of oil peaking would otherwise be chaotic. The experiences of the 1970s and 1980s offer important guides as to government actions that are desirable and those that are undesirable, but the process will not be easy.

adjustment periods may be of little immediate concern to oil producers and energy traders—indeed, higher prices are necessary to spur investments in new production—but they are of serious concern to the households, industries, and governments that face real economic and human costs as a result.

FedEx CEO Frederick Smith and retired U.S. General P.X. Kelley summed up the problem in a recent op-ed for the *Washington Post*:

> *Pure market economics will never solve this problem. Markets do not account for the hidden and indirect costs of oil dependence. Businesses focused on the highest return on investment are not always in a position to implement new solutions, many of which depend on technologies and fuels that cannot currently compete with the marginal cost of producing a barrel of oil.*
>
> *Most important of all, the marketplace alone will not act preemptively to mitigate the enormous damage that would be inflicted by a sudden, serious and sustained price increase. Government leadership is absolutely necessary.*
>
> *- Smith, F. and Kelley, P.X. "Are we ready for the next oil shock?" The Washington Post, 11 Aug 2006.*

The inability of markets to adequately address a problem with such serious potential economic and social consequences means that government leadership is necessary.

We can no longer assume that the global economy will continually provide affordable oil in the short term, and develop acceptable alternatives in the long term. Moreover, the actions needed to substantially reduce global (and national) economic dependence on oil require many years of planning and implementation (see *Box 2* above). The inability of markets to adequately address a problem with such serious potential economic and social consequences means that government leadership is necessary.

Because we have high demand at the moment, this is what creates price volatility. It could be disruption from many areas, like refining, transport or production...It is not just one area but all of them combined. This tightness means there is no cushion in the marketplace if anything goes wrong.

- Muhammed Ali Zainy, Centre of Global Energy Studies. "No escape from oil price volatility," Aljazeera.net, 9 June 2005

3. Local Challenges, Local Advantages

Every municipality is uniquely defined by its local history, charter, politics, culture, tax base, demographics, environment and any number of other factors. And every community will face some unique challenges when confronting peak oil and global warming.

Much has been published over the last twenty years about the threat of global warming and the actions that governments, businesses and households can take to reduce their greenhouse gas emissions. In contrast, peak oil and the challenges it poses to our economies and communities is little understood. In light of this imbalance in available information, this section focuses mostly on energy uncertainty, and covers the following:

— the ways in which energy uncertainty challenges cities of all sizes,

— the responsibilities and advantages local governments have for addressing theses challenges,

— the other local, regional, and national actors which impact local government operations, and

— the leadership challenges involved in local governments addressing such complex and large-scale issues.

3.1 **The challenges our cities face** In its most basic sense, energy uncertainty means we don't know what the future holds for energy prices, and we don't know how these changing prices will effect the global economy over time. For local governments—responsible for managing local public services, planning for future land use and transportation, and protecting the community's economic and social health—this uncertainty creates a wide variety of risks and vulnerabilities.

Elected officials and planners should take a four-part approach to addressing both energy and climate uncertainty:

> **Mayors are very concerned about the recent spike in fuel and energy costs and the financial burden it places on American citizens and their families. We know that aggressive action is necessary to turn this tide, and we are taking the lead in addressing the nation's energy challenges to reduce our dependency on foreign oil. We cannot wait on the federal government; we must do what mayors do best and act now.**
>
> – Mayor Beverly O'Neill (Long Beach, California), President, United States Conference of Mayors, 10 May 2006.

Challenges and Advantages

- **Identify local changes and local vulnerabilities** that have been brought about by energy and climate uncertainty, or that may arise in the future.

- **Mitigate local vulnerabilities** while contributing to broader efforts that are mitigating peak oil and climate change at a global level.

- **Prepare for potential problems in the short term**, such as extreme weather events and sudden fuel shortages.

- **Plan for long-term changes** that cannot be avoided, minimizing the disruption they will cause and taking advantage of the opportunities they will offer.

Each of these steps has its own set of challenges, but identifying changes and vulnerabilities is particularly difficult because it requires inquiry into some of the most fundamental—and complex—systems that support our communities. We'll focus on vulnerabilities in this chapter, and look at mitigation and planning in subsequent chapters.

What are the most urgent vulnerabilities?

The Portland (Oregon) Peak Oil Task Force, an ad hoc body of citizen and business leaders appointed by the Portland City Council in May 2006, studied the potential impacts of peak oil and recommend strategies the city could implement in response. The task force spent over six months researching their community's provisioning and support systems, consulting with over 80 stakeholders in the process.

In its March 2007 final report—the most comprehensive local government-sponsored assessment to date of the local challenges related to peak oil—the task force identified 27 specific impacts and vulnerabilities (see *Box 3. Local Impacts and Vulnerabilities, Portland (Ore.) Peak Oil Task Force*). Although this list was developed specifically for the Portland context, is gives an indication of the kinds of vulnerabilities any locality can expect to find.

3.2 Understanding the complexity of energy uncertainty
Overlapping, intertwined issues

Portland, Oregon, may at first appear to be the kind of community that should fare reasonably well as oil becomes more expensive:

- It has made extensive investments in diversifying its transportation system, so that more people bicycle, walk and use public transit relative to most other U.S. cities.

- Locally-grown produce is relatively abundant and affordable thanks to a proliferation of farmers markets and an urban growth boundary that keeps farms from being swallowed up by suburban sprawl.

- The City government aggressively and successfully promotes sustainable practices like green building, the use of biofuels and construction waste recycling through a well-regarded Office of Sustainable Development.

And yet, Portland could fare *worse* than other U.S. cities in an oil-scarce future because, as the air, rail and trucking hub of its region, its economy happens to be particularly tied to trade and transportation. Should Portland therefore plan for increased demand for services because of future in-migration, or for rising unemployment and population loss because of a future decline in shipping and travel?

We don't know—we can't know, because the factors and systems in play are too complex. For Portland to intelligently plan its future, it would need a nuanced strategy that recognizes uncertainty and complexity, and self-adjusts in response to changing conditions. It would make no sense to just choose one of many likely scenarios of energy prices and economic behaviors, extend this into the future and plan accordingly. And yet, this is exactly what conventional planning methods do: they tend to assume that the future will not be much different than the past (see *Box 4. Energy and land use / transportation planning*).

Assessing vulnerabilities related to energy uncertainty is a much more involved task than simply writing down the ways that a municipal program uses fuel. Because oil and natural gas are the most important raw materials to modern society, a significant change in their price or availability will have ripple effects throughout the economy that are difficult to predict. As we'll see below, these ripple effects can create swift impacts in unlikely places.

It's an enormous undertaking. It really is staggering, to recognize just what [Peak Oil] means for society as a whole, and in particular your own jurisdiction.

– Councilmember Dave Rollo, City of Bloomington, Indiana

To simply relegate energy planning to a nice tidy chapter where we promote solar panels and biofuels, while turning around and promulgating the same old tired assumptions of growth-dependent, auto-centric, single use zoning does a great disservice to our allegedly 'forward looking' profession and society in general.

- Patrick Ford, Planner, Mendocino County, California

Box 3   Local Impacts and Vulnerabilities, Portland (Ore.) Peak Oil Task Force

Summarized from "Descending the Oil Peak: Navigating the Transition from Oil and Natural Gas," Portland (Oregon) Peak Oil Task Force, March 2007; available online at http://www.portlandonline.com/osd. See the complete report for a full description of each identified impact.

Impacts on Transportation and Land Use

T1. Automobile use will decline and people will seek alternative transportation for their needs.

T2. People and businesses will relocate to be closer to each other and to transportation options; population will likely shift to city centers, and density and mixed-use development will increase.

T3. Transportation of freight will become more costly, likely leading to mode shifts from air and truck to rail and boat.

T4. Air travel may decline significantly.

T5. Maintenance of road infrastructure will be increasingly difficult because of loss of revenue and reliance on asphalt.

Impacts on Food and Agriculture

F1. The amount and variety of food produced will decrease.

F2. Food will cost more.

F3. Low-income households are most vulnerable to higher prices and could see a decline in diet and nutrition.

F4. The kinds of foods produced and processed will shift, introducing business pressures and opportunities for food producers and processors.

F5. Households will experience increased pressure to grow, process and handle their own food.

F6. Food retailing options will shift.

F7. There will be less food waste and changes in packaging.

Impacts on Business, Economy and Jobs

E1. Prices will rise, and the number of business start-ups and failures will increase.

E2. Some businesses will experience significantly higher production and distribution costs; others may be more impacted by changes in demand for their products and services.

E3. Unemployment will likely increase in the short term.

E4. Impacts will vary in intensity by industry and business division.

E5. Portland's population may grow faster than forecast as a result of in-migration.

Impacts on Public and Social Services

S1. Vulnerable and marginalized populations will grow and will be the first and hardest hit by peak oil.

S2. Increasing costs and decreasing incomes will reduce health coverage and further stress the health care system, a system already in crisis.

S3. Protection of public health will be at increased risk.

S4. Demand for social services will increase, but the ability to provide service will decline.

S5. Heating, maintenance and monthly housing costs will consume a larger share of household budgets and push people toward lower-quality housing choices.

S6. Demand for public school services may increase at the same time that costs of maintaining public school facilities increase.

S7. It is unclear whether demand for electricity will increase or decrease; electric loads served by natural gas-fired generation will have to be reduced or replaced by renewable energy.

S8. First responders, especially police, may become primary service providers as social services struggle to meet demand.

S9. Water, sewer and solid waste services are not expected to be affected significantly.

S10. Competitive, individualistic responses could erode community spirit and cohesion.

Box 4   Energy and land use / transportation planning

Land use and transportation planners rely heavily on economic forecasts and models to inform decisions about future transportation and development needs. Public investments in transportation infrastructure, public-private partnerships for large real estate development projects, and comprehensive Town Plans (zoning laws and general community development goals) are all based on the ability of planners to reasonably predict where people and businesses will locate in a region and how they will move about that region five, fifteen, even thirty years in the future.

These forecasts generally assume relative stability in macroeconomic factors like labor supply, national monetary policy, income distribution, consumption patterns, and of course energy prices. Planners extend long-term trends into the future, with the assumption that in twenty years the fundamentals will not be radically different than they are today.

But what happens if a long-term trend like stable fuel prices changes? Planners' assumptions about fuel prices directly affect their assumptions about transportation mode split (the split of all trips in a geographic area across different modes of transportation, such as private automobile, public transportation, bicycle and walking): mode split is largely determined by income[26] and by trip price, which itself is largely a function of fuel price. If we expect that fuel prices won't change radically in the future, we will assume that mode splits won't change radically either.

Such assumptions about stable future mode splits have been reasonable and accurate for decades. With the exception of the oil crises in the 1970s, the cost of motor fuel in the U.S. and Canada has rarely exhibited serious volatility since World War II, and never for a long period of time. These assumptions could create serious problems, however, should the price of fuel radically change in the future.

At a high enough sustained fuel price, we can expect households and firms to change their travel behaviors for economic reasons. If extended oil price volatility starts to fundamentally shift mode split, transportation planners may no longer be able to reasonably predict transportation patterns beyond a relatively short time frame. Were this the case, it could be significantly more difficult to make well-informed decisions in the present about investing hundreds of millions of dollars for future transportation projects. The difficulties also extend to land use planning, because land use patterns are closely related to transportation patterns, as well as to local, regional and national economic trends.

It's not at all clear how planning forecasts and models might address this problem of assuming the inevitability of long-term energy trends. A recent survey[27] of widely-used transportation engineering texts and state-of-the-art transportation modeling techniques found that they generally do not consider energy constraints at all.

So what do we know about how land use and transportation patterns might change as oil prices rise and become volatile? Not surprisingly, some land use studies[28] of the 1970s oil crises suggest that consistently high oil prices would cause centrally-located land to increase in value as households and firms try to reduce travel costs. This could very well mean that the high and volatile oil prices which are expected to accompany peak oil will encourage more people and businesses to move into downtowns and other more central, dense urban areas.

However, these studies also note that the forces driving metropolitan decentralization are very strong and not easily counteracted. Much depends on how governments and businesses respond to these long-term changes with planning, policy and actual investments.

High oil prices, higher asphalt prices

In the summer of 2006 many municipalities in the U.S. and Canada found that they couldn't complete planned street maintenance projects because costs had skyrocketed (see *Box 5. Oil prices and street maintenance costs*). Higher oil prices were the main cause, but the effect was disproportionate: crude oil only rose approximately 5% from mid-2005 to mid-2006, yet the cost of asphalt doubled, and street maintenance costs in some regions tripled. What happened?

Asphalt is a byproduct of refining oil for fuels. When oil prices started rising beyond normal levels in 2004, and especially after Hurricane Katrina reduced Gulf of Mexico production in September 2005, the base cost of asphalt rose. At the same time, high oil prices meant that refineries had incentive to produce more higher-revenue products per barrel of oil, and thus less asphalt; refineries make much more money from the gasoline and diesel they produce out of a barrel of oil than from the asphalt.

Together with continued high demand for asphalt from booming construction in many parts of the U.S. and Canada, asphalt supply was squeezed and prices rose even further. Street construction took a double hit from rising oil prices because it requires not only asphalt but significant amounts of fuel for moving machinery and asphalt on site and for keeping the asphalt hot before it is laid.

This jump in street maintenance costs had multiple effects:

- Many jurisdictions had to change their paving plans, from scaling back and postponing to canceling them altogether.

- Postponed and canceled projects meant less work for crews and less revenue for paving companies.

- Reduced work and revenue meant less pay or no pay for paving crews, and ultimately less in income and business taxes to governments.

- Less road construction and road maintenance meant that transportation infrastructure improvements were delayed, at a cost of more expensive future repairs. It may have also meant delays for real estate development projects that depended on the construction or repair of streets.

The vulnerability of municipal street maintenance to oil price changes is an instructive example of how even a relatively small change in the supply and price of oil can have many unexpected effects. It's also an example of why planning for oil price volatility needs to happen at the local level: impacts were felt differently throughout the U.S. and Canada thanks to local differences in construction activity, budgeting (some jurisdictions planned for cost hikes, others didn't), and regional variations of asphalt and fuel themselves. Even similarly-sized towns in the same region may have had different experiences.

See *Systems Thinking: A Tool for Municipalities* in the Appendix for an exploration of how a street maintenance program might be seen in relation to larger governmental and economic systems, and what can be learned from this approach.

For instance, Hamblen County [Tenn.], a typical Renfro [Construction Co.] customer, could not afford any paving this year. Road Superintendent Barry Poole said high asphalt prices 'really put us out of the ballgame' in an already tight budget year.

'Here was a job we were counting on for $400,000 to $500,000 worth of work, and all of a sudden it's zero,' said Renfro's [senior vice president, Robert] Hill.

Hill said Renfro has had to lay off truck drivers and paving crews in order to stay competitive.

- Eder, Andrew, "High price of asphalt puts brakes on paving projects," Knoxville News Sentinel [Tenn.], 6 Sept. 2006

Box 5 Oil prices and street maintenance costs

In the summer of 2006, crude oil prices has risen 5% over the previous summer, but the price of asphalt more than doubled. Municipalities across the U.S. and Canada struggled to cope with these unexpected costs for street maintenance:

Lowell Prange, administrator for the City of Menomonie [Wisc.], said that as the largest user, the public works department is affected most by the increase in fuel prices.... 'We'll see what happens next year, because that was a pretty big bump, and it takes a big hit out of your budget when you got to go up by $50,000 to $60,000 in a $10 million dollar budget. It takes away from what the city can do, or fund'.

- Ryder, Sarah, "Rising fuel costs wreak havoc on local budgets." The Dunn County News [Wisconsin], 7 Sept. 2006

Though Ontario cities have managed to cope so far, that's likely to change. Toronto signed the bulk of its paving contracts early in the year, when the cost of asphalt was low, but there are concerns that plans for next year will have to be modified when new contracts are signed at higher prices.

'Probably we will not be able to resurface and possibly even reconstruct the same number of roads we originally expected,' said Gary Welsh, the city's manager for transportation services. 'It probably wouldn't affect any of the high-priority projects, but there may be some local resurfacing projects [postponed or scaled back].'

- Sethi, Chanakya, "High cost of asphalt steamrolls plans." The Globe and Mail [Toronto], 26 June 2006

The agency has sold roughly $150 million in bonds the last 10 years in its effort to provide sewer service citywide. But it has lost money recently as rising oil prices have sent construction prices skyrocketing, particularly on PVC pipe and asphalt, said John Martin, manager of billing services.

'If we continue this now with the prices escalating, we're just going to go into a deeper hole,' Martin said.

- Barbarisi, Daniel. "Rising construction costs put Sewer Authority in fiscal hole." The Providence Journal [Rhode Island], Tuesday, 8 Aug. 2006

High price of asphalt puts brakes on paving projects

J. MILES CARY/NEWS SENTINEL

Workers pave part of Interstate 40 in downtown Knoxville in this July 2001 photo. The high price of asphalt means state and local governments are pursuing fewer road projects these days. Bruce Wuethrich, senior director of engineering and public works for Knox County, said the county has not had to sacrifice capital projects — the building of new roads or major reconstruction projects that generally cost more than $50,000. Instead, it has scaled back maintenance projects in subdivisions.

County hasn't quit new roads but halts maintenance work

BY ANDREW EDER
edera@knews.com

When Knox County awarded a bid for a road-resurfacing project near the beginning of the year, the price of asphalt was holding steady after a post-Hurricane Katrina spike.

But by the time paving began two months later, the project cost shot up about 40 percent.

"It turned out to be 20 miles of road that got bumped off the paving list," said Bruce Wuethrich, senior director of engineering and public works for the county. "The worst effect was my street got knocked off the paving list."

Liquid asphalt is a petroleum byproduct produced mainly in oil refineries. The dark, viscous substance is combined with materials like gravel, crushed rock and sand, or aggregate, to produce asphalt pavement.

Construction materials have been rising in price across the board since Hurricane Katrina last year. But liquid asphalt has seen an especially sharp rise, nearly doubling during the past 12 months.

That spike in price has put the squeeze on paving contractors, and it means state and local governments are pursuing fewer road projects.

Wuethrich said Knox County has not had to sacrifice capital projects — the building of new roads or major reconstruction proj-

ON KNOXNEWS.COM

■ Take a virtual tour of an asphalt plant

■ See a detailed table and chart of historical asphalt prices

ects that generally cost more than $50,000. Instead, it has scaled back maintenance projects in subdivisions. The 20 miles of road cut from the paving list were all residential, he noted.

Tom Clabo, chief civil engineer for the city of Knoxville, said rising asphalt prices have pushed back a paving project that was approved in July.

"We're delaying letting that project until early 2007 to see if prices come back down," he said. "If that liquid asphalt price doesn't come down, we'll be in the same situation as the county."

Counting the cost

Statewide, the Tennessee Department of Transportation this year will let about 36 fewer resurfacing contracts, including interstate projects, said spokeswoman Kim Keelor.

Robert Hill, senior vice president of Renfro Construction, said the cost of liquid asphalt has basically doubled in a year — from about $200 per liquid ton a year ago to the current price of about $400 per liquid ton.

See **ASPHALT** on C4

DID YOU KNOW?

Asphalt cement is a dark, viscous material found in crude petroleum. The cement is separated out in the oil refining process and transported to a plant near the paving site. Asphalt cement is mixed with hard material called aggregate to form asphalt concrete, also called blacktop. Asphalt pavement consists of a surface layer of asphalt concrete over several layers of other materials. Asphalt pavement is the most recycled product in the country, with 80 percent of removed pavement being reused in new paving projects.

Source: National Asphalt Pavement Association

HISTORICAL ASPHALT PRICES

■ **Sept. 2006:** $391.15/ton
■ **July 2006:** $377.31/ton
■ **April 2006:** $278.75/ton
■ **Jan. 2006:** $239.17/ton
■ **Sept. 2005:** $227.08/ton
■ **Aug. 2005:** $199.17/ton
■ **Jan. 2005:** $189.58/ton

Source: Tennessee Department of Transportation Bituminous Index

Eder, Andrew, "High price of asphalt puts brakes on paving projects," Knoxville News Sentinel [Tenn.], 6 Sept. 2006

Responding at the local level
Why municipal action?

There are four important reasons why municipalities should respond to energy and climate uncertainty, and not wait for state/provincial or federal agencies to act first:

- **It is in every municipality's best economic interest.**
  Virtually everything that cities do to respond to energy and climate uncertainty will save them money in the long run. More energy-efficient buildings, more locally-controlled energy sources, and more compact and transit-oriented land uses are all ultimately fiscally conservative and energy-prudent goals to pursue. In addition to saving money, those communities that are less vulnerable to the effects of peak oil and climate change will have a economic advantage over communities that are ill-prepared.

- **Higher level governments cannot see the details that local governments can.**
  In the Introduction we mentioned how a number of North Carolina municipalities unexpectedly found themselves without motor fuels after two pipelines were shut down due to Hurricane Katrina. While the State had an energy coordination office, it wasn't necessarily looking out to make sure that Smalltown, North Carolina in particular would have the fuels they needed following an emergency. And in fact, you wouldn't really expect them to: at the level of a state agency, officials need to think at the scale of regional supply chains and hundreds or thousands of municipalities.

- **There is often a time lag for responses from higher level governments.**
  This makes the local government a kind of "first responder" to all local issues. Whether the problem is within the realm of a municipality's responsibilities or not, local citizens and businesses will turn to local officials and local resources first in times of emergency. For example, state/provincial and federal programs exist to help people heat their homes, and to help local agencies run winterization programs. But in any given winter month, if a family suddenly can't afford a new delivery of heating oil, or there's a problem with local natural gas distribution (which has happened recently in other countries in Europe and South America), it's the local government that must deal with the repercussions first.

> A municipal government, with its local experts, local accountability, local information and local interests has the flexibility, capacity and motivation to address issues in ways that larger governments cannot.

- **Municipalities are uniquely suited to meet certain societal needs.**
  A municipal government, with its local experts, local accountability, local information and, most especially, local interests at heart, has the flexibility, capacity and motivation to address issues in ways that larger governments cannot. This is why communities usually have local jurisdiction over the things that are most important to us, like schools, police and land uses (albeit within a framework established by higher level governments). This same thinking should apply to the vulnerabilities and risks our communities face in energy and climate uncertainty.

The advantages of the local level

How can local governments hope to address energy and climate uncertainty with smaller budgets, fewer staff, and less institutional expertise than state, provincial and federal governments? In the U.S. and Canada, local governments have two important advantages: a set of key municipal powers, and direct relationships with the decision-makers and resources in their communities.

Challenges and Advantages

Municipal powers

Local governments in the U.S. and Canada can have a large range of official responsibilities, from providing basic services like water, police and schools, to implementing long-term plans for future land use and transportation patterns. Through these responsibilities and powers, they have influence over three areas of urban spatial and economic development that are essential for addressing energy consumption and carbon emissions:

- **Building construction and energy efficiency**
  Municipalities can influence how buildings are built through zoning codes, building codes and the permitting process. This power provides quite a bit of control over how buildings contribute to the community's energy demand and carbon emissions. Local governments can boost requirements for building insulation, allow building owners to install energy-generating devices, encourage building designs that save energy and encourage walking, discourage building designs that waste energy... the possibilities are vast.

- **Local land use and transportation patterns**
  Municipalities create plans to guide and regulate the development of land and the construction of transportation infrastructure. Land use and transportation planning decisions have great influence on whether community businesses and households will be completely dependent on private cars for meeting basic needs, or will have a choice of modes and the possibility of saving energy.

- **Local economic activity**
  Municipalities work to nurture local economic health in various ways, such as enabling public-private development projects with public bonds and tax incentives or collaborating with the local business community on city marketing. These and other local government activities are all opportunities to encourage development in a low-energy, zero-carbon direction, by incentive or example or both.

In addition to powers of influence, most U.S. and Canadian municipalities also wield considerable spending power: they collect local, state/provincial and federal funds, and then disburse funds to provide local services and make capital investments. Rather than wait for surpluses to fund new initiatives, municipal leaders can use existing disbursements as leverage to meet changing municipal goals. For example, a scheduled department expenditure to renovate a building presents an opportunity to retrofit that building for better energy efficiency. Or at a much larger scale, a project funded by a big federal community development grant may present an opportunity to pursue a neighborhood heat/power cogeneration facility[29] with a private partner.

Direct relationship with the local community

The daily operations of local government are deeply entwined with local personal and business relationships, years of shared memory and history, and the shared experience of place among the people who live and work there.

Municipal leaders are part of their communities: they use the same roads that they build, their kids often go to the same schools that they administer, and they are neighbors with the same people who pay their salaries and/or vote them into (or out of) office. With countless personal connections among citizens, business leaders, community leaders and municipal staff comes an intimate familiarity with the community and the way it works that is invaluable and irreplaceable.

Municipalities have a responsibility to investigate how their communities may be vulnerable to high and volatile oil prices, and to develop their own plans for mitigating risks.

This local familiarity underscores municipalities' responsibility to their communities to investigate how they may be vulnerable to high and volatile oil prices, and develop their own plans for mitigating risks.

3.4 **Reaching out beyond City Hall** Whether a "contract city" outsourcing common services or a full-service bureaucracy, all municipal governments discharge their responsibilities within a unique context of local, regional and national actors and influences. It's important for leaders to recognize the **resources** and **challenges** this context presents for addressing any issue, but this is especially true when addressing a complex system problem like energy and climate uncertainty.

Resources for addressing municipal issues abound outside City Hall, and can be particularly valuable for smaller communities where municipal staff are often stretched thin. Local citizen and business groups are resources for local knowledge, professional expertise and volunteer labor. Non-profit organizations, university research centers and national associations offer trainings, conferences and publications where municipal officials and staff can learn about best practices and new developments. Many higher-level governments and utilities have incentive programs to assist municipal and business investments in energy efficiency and alternative fuel technology.

At the same time, actors at different scales may present challenges to addressing energy and climate uncertainty at the local level. Federal and state/provincial regulations may preclude certain kinds of local initiatives. Associations and organizations may pursue programs or legislation that run counter to municipal goals. Local citizens and businesses may oppose their tax dollars being spent on an issue that seems beyond the scope of municipal government.

Leaders who recognize these resources and challenges will be better equipped to develop strategies to cope with energy and climate uncertainty. This is both a political reality and a very practical strategy for an issue affecting municipal interests in ways that no one person or even one agency can hope to fully identify and manage alone.

Local context

The local government is only one of many institutions in most communities, and is often not even the largest or most powerful. Experienced municipal leaders know well that their regulatory and spending power is ultimately limited by the support they are able to develop among local stakeholders, from the business and real estate development communities to ethnic and religious communities.

The actors in your community are resources for local knowledge, ideas, volunteer efforts, skills, and access to yet other actors for resources. As individuals, they already have a direct relationship with the municipality as voters and taxpayers, and for many, also as volunteers for advisory committees, safety teams, and community events. Finally, they are the "customers" of municipal government, expecting certain services, good judgment, responsible planning, and accountability.

- **Municipal staff and officials**

  The city lives or dies by the work of its employees, from the accountants to the planners to the sewer maintenance crew. It's the staff working with municipal systems day after day who are often the first to recognize where vulnerabilities exist, or where efficiencies could be gained. After the elected official who initiated a new program has finished her term, it's municipal staff who will continue running it.

  Just as importantly, the best ideas from staff usually go nowhere if upper management and officials are not on board. Elected officials in particular are often loath to embrace a new idea for municipal action, and generally will not risk possible political damage until they feel personally excited and supported on an idea. Municipal leaders do well to engage staff and citizens regularly to both solicit and discuss ideas.

  Certain staff and officials will provide essential input to addressing energy and climate uncertainty. Talk about the effects of oil price changes with your land use planners, transportation planners, and traffic engineers; they may each have different ideas

Challenges and Advantages

When Mia Birk was hired to lead a new Bicycle Program for the City of Portland, one of the first things she did was accompany the street maintenance crews on their overnight shifts.

I said 'OK, teach me what you guys do. How do you maintain the system? What does it take to replace a drainage grate with a bike-friendly grate? What are the issues, the costs, the problems?' I brought doughnuts.

Then later I sat down with all of them and said, 'OK, here's the problem that has been identified...I have some ideas, but what suggestions do you guys have?' And there were some guys who were ambivalent, but with a lot of them we were able to start coming up with ideas, and we improved the system.

- Mia Birk, Alta Planning + Design, Portland, Oregon

about the future of oil, but they will also each have valuable insights that will contribute to the picture of your municipality's vulnerabilities.

- **Business Community**
  The local economy is the backbone of the municipality, making the business community one of the most important forces to consider in local governance. From individual firms concerned about rising energy costs to business associations like the local Chamber of Commerce or Kiwanis Club, the business community is an important reservoir of leadership, local knowledge, practical expertise and financial resources.[30]

  The local real estate development community is a particularly important partner for addressing energy and climate uncertainty. Developers, financers, architects and contractors are the key decision-makers in what actually gets built—and how it gets built—in a city. The construction of buildings and the larger land use and transportation patterns they create are some of the biggest factors in a community's overall local energy use. Throughout the U.S. and Canada, real estate developers are increasingly embracing ideas like "smart growth", green building and transit-oriented development as good business decisions that also make for more livable and energy-smart communities.

- **Civil community**
  Citizens vote and pay taxes, but they also volunteer with community efforts, lead civic organizations, and even start political initiatives to do things they don't see government and business leaders doing. The civil community includes formal associations that specifically work for community betterment, such as parent-school associations, neighborhood associations, social service non-profits and citizen action committees. As we'll see in Section 4.1, citizen groups have been key players in some of the recent municipal initiatives to address peak oil.

  Many membership-driven groups also engage regularly with civic interests, such as Boy Scouts and Girl Scouts, fraternal organizations and many faith communities. Strong ethnic communities also often have formal or informal civic-minded association; even homeowner associations and assisted-living communities sometimes pursue civic functions beyond their immediate living situations.

- **Educational institutions**
  Some of the most valuable resources for a municipality reside in its educational and cultural institutions. Grade schools, with their publicly-owned physical plant and deep connections to their surrounding communities, present opportunities for new programs and citizen communication and involvement. Colleges and universities were among the first institutional organizations to adopt sustainability programs, and every year more schools initiate programs or research on energy and sustainability.

- **Other governmental bodies**
  Neighboring jurisdictions, special service districts, county government and other locally-oriented organizations in your area can be important partners for addressing big issues like transportation, land use and energy supply.

State/Provincial and regional context

States in the U.S. and provinces in Canada both possess all powers not otherwise designated by their respective federal Constitutions, explicitly including powers of land use regulation. A "region," on the other hand, can mean a county, a metropolitan area, a collection of municipalities in a remote area, or something else entirely, depending on the area of the U.S. or Canada.

In both countries, states and provinces are the bodies that charter local governments and bestow on them their own regulatory power over land use, public utilities and other responsibilities. In the U.S., many municipalities receive significant funding from their state government. Many non-governmental bodies also operate at the regional and state/provincial levels, including universities, associations and advocacy organizations.

- **United States: Regional planning and governance**
  True regional government is virtually non-existent in the United States.[31] U.S. counties serve multiple municipalities, but rarely function as actual multi-jurisdictional coordinating bodies, and instead tend to provide certain city-like services such as police, human services, roads and parks to non-city areas. Furthermore, in many urban areas, counties are too small to encompass the entire metropolitan region.

  The only regional governmental body found consistently throughout the United States is the metropolitan planning organization (MPO), which tends to be limited to coordinating regional transportation planning and acts as the conduit for bringing federal transportation funds to local and regional projects. MPOs vary in power across the country, but all provide one of the few formal opportunities in the U.S. system for local leaders to meet regularly. Also, because of their focus on transportation, MPOs are a natural forum for addressing issues surrounding energy use.

  Various other associative regional bodies exist as state and local leaders have seen fit to establish them. These include Regional Councils, Associations/Councils of Governments, Regional Planning and Development Districts, Planning Councils and other unelected bodies, some acting as the region's MPO and some simply serving as a forum for elected officials.

- **Canada: Regional planning and governance**
  Regional-level governance is somewhat more organized in Canada, although forms also vary across the country, from the multi-jurisdictional "regional districts" of British Columbia to the "regional municipality" city-county hybrids in Nova Scotia and Ontario. Regional bodies may provide "municipal" functions over a larger area in situations where it's more economically or logistically preferable to do so, including land use planning, environmental protection and other public services. They also can function as forums for local government partnerships.

- **United States: State Energy Offices**
  In the United States, some of the most important state-level bodies for energy issues are the State Energy Offices, largely funded by the federal State Energy Program established in 1996 by the consolidation of the State Energy Conservation Program (SECP) and the Institutional Conversation Program (ICP). State Energy Offices generally exist to provide advice on energy issues to state officials, promote energy efficiency and conservation, manage certain federal energy research programs and assist utilities and consumers during energy emergencies.

- **Canada: Provincial energy issues**
  Every province addresses energy production and consumption issues in its own way. For example, energy efficiency programs are run in Nova Scotia by the Department of Environment and Labor, in Québec by the Ministry of Natural Resources and Wildlife, in Ontario by the Ministry of Energy, in Alberta by the Office of Utilities Consumer Advocate, and in British Columbia by the Ministry of Energy, Mines and Petroleum Resources. The scope and goals of each program also vary widely.

- **Port Authorities**
  Port authorities (also known as port districts) are major quasi-governmental regional actors responsible for coordinating and encouraging port development, including trucking, shipping, rail and air. They are extremely involved in regional trade and freight transportation issues, of course, but also in local economy and local environmental issues. In both the U.S. and Canada, port authorities are usually governed by a board appointed by local, state/provincial and federal officials.

Challenges and Advantages

• **State/Provincial municipal leagues**
Every state and province has some kind of association or league of municipalities, sometimes multiple associations (for example, urban municipalities and rural municipalities). State/Provincial level associations of public officials, managers and employees are also common.

National context

National-level factors, from federal government policies and programs to the national economy itself, have indirect but strong influences on how municipalities and their communities function.

The most noteworthy national-level associations of city governments are the National League of Cities in the U.S. and the Federation of Canadian Municipalities in Canada. Both advocate for municipal interests at a national level, and provide extensive resources and programs for local government needs, including technical assistance and 'best practices' databases. Other, more specialized associations also exist, such as the National Association of Towns and Townships (U.S.), which focuses on federal lobbying for smaller communities.

Equally active are associations of municipal leaders and employees, most notably the International City/County Management Association, the U.S. Conference of Mayors and the Canadian Association of Municipal Administrators. Numerous organizations also operate at the national level on just about every issue municipalities may work with, from transportation and energy to recycling and sewage treatment. See *Appendix: Resources* for a full list of organizations and their websites.

3.5 **Leadership** Frank and Deborah Popper, two professors from New Jersey, traveled to the Great Plains in 1987 to present their research on long-term population and economic decline in Kansas, Nebraska and other states. When they proposed their solution of abandoning parts of those declining regions to create a new national "Buffalo Commons," local residents were outraged, and Kansas Governor Mike Hayden famously responded, "Tell the Poppers that America's Great Plains do not equal the Sahara."

Seventeen years later, to a packed house at Kansas State University, Governor Hayden shocked everyone with a public reversal: "I was wrong. Not only did what Frank and Deborah predict come true, but the truth is the outmigration of the Great Plains and the depopulation and aging of the population has been stronger, in many quarters, than what they predicted."[32]

Why was there such a visceral local reaction to mere statistics and a crazy idea from some East Coast academics? Why did it take 17 years for a local leader to stand up and publicly acknowledge what had become clear as day?

Decline is difficult to accept, especially in our economic system that expects, and to a large degree even depends, on growth. In fact, decline is just as normal as growth, and is to be expected as part of the regular economic cycle: the only U.S. regions that have never shown signs of decline at some point in history are the Mid-Atlantic and the Southwest[33]. Yet we don't prepare for decline: city planners aren't taught how to "plan for decline," and it would be the courageous politician indeed who ran on a platform of "accepting decline."

Much like population or economic decline, the specter of oil and natural gas scarcity threatens our way of life. As individuals, our immediate response is to deny it, to find some reason to dismiss it. For elected officials, peak oil is even less appealing to accept: "How could I even begin to approach such a complex issue? Is it an issue that I can do anything about? If I speak out on this issue, how will it affect my re-election chances?"

Publicly talking about peak oil and global warming is no easy task for local elected officials and city staff. Part of the Great Plains communities' challenge in addressing long-term change was the reality that, in the short-term or in any one locality, the change may not have been apparent, or may not have seemed as deep-seated as it really was. As Deborah Popper put it "How do you recognize when there's long term structural change? How do you recognize whether it's anomalous, or a straight-line trend, or if we're just bouncing around?"[34]

These are difficult questions, but they are the kinds of questions that communities expect their leaders and elected officials to ask.

Leadership within local government

Recognizing peak oil and global warming is hard enough—then there's the challenge of *addressing* them. Most jurisdictions do not have extra resources available to devote staff time to addressing such long term issues. It is vitally important as a municipal response strategy to get officials and staff to integrate energy and climate uncertainty into their regular work. This can happen easily by raising awareness about the issue among staff: announcements and presentations are important, as are workshops, scenario role-plays, and other interactive methods that encourage individuals to ask themselves how their specific roles relate to energy and climate uncertainty.

The kinds of questions different actors within municipal government might ask themselves will vary. For example:

- **Elected Officials**

    –What is it that my jurisdiction should be responsible for, and what does the community expect me to be responsible for?

    –What is it that will be regarded by my constituents as a responsible thing to do?

    –Who in the community outside the local government should we be bringing in to these discussions?

- **Managers / Policy Advisors**

    –What assumptions are we making within our department about the price and availability of oil and natural gas?

    –How can we make sure that we're learning about vulnerabilities and opportunities from staff, and communicating them to the right people?

- **Planners / Technicians**

    –If our jurisdiction is going to be compatible with efforts to respond to oil/gas scarcity, what are the kinds of things that we should be thinking about?

    –What's the planning and engineering thought process that goes along with this?

- **Operations Managers and Staff**

    –What are we doing that we might have to do differently if oil, natural gas, electricity, or gasoline became more expensive?

    –What's easy to change—and what's not easy to change—to reduce our exposure to higher prices?

We should pursue strategies that are conservative and iterative, closely monitor the results of new initiatives, and regularly re-assesses context and potential impacts.

The task before municipalities is large, but not impossible. Both governments and communities have past experience managing resource constraints of one form or another. It often takes a crisis or imminent threat to spur action, however; the challenge with energy and climate uncertainty, then, will be to spur preparatory actions within municipal government before a crisis turns the future problem into a present emergency.

Leadership for complexity

How can we create meaningful plans for significant changes that we cannot easily predict? One relatively new method of planning for uncertainty—"adaptive management"—comes from the environmental sciences.

Adaptive management was born out of the failures of conventional management practices like those that contributed to the collapse of the North Atlantic cod fishery in the 1990s. Adaptive management recognizes that natural resources make up—and are made up of—

It's so easy not to talk about [peak oil], there's this kind of vacuum of silence on this complex issue. It's a comfortable space, no one's really pressing [politicians] to do it.

And there's all kinds of reasons why you don't have to. You're not going to be changing the geopolitics of oil — you, a municipal councilor, right? You probably can't even change some of the fundamentals in your own region! And yet you have to give people some kind of hope, you have to recognize their aspirations.

– Gordon Price, former City Councilor, Vancouver, British Columbia

I think a key thing in almost every city I work in that's very successful is the really good people that have really good relationships with everybody throughout the department, people who just understand that establishing those relationships is a big part of their job.

– Mia Birk, Alta Planning + Design, Portland, Oregon

Box 6 Learning from related approaches

Urban Design: "New Urbanism" and "Smart Growth"

One of the biggest developments in U.S. and Canadian urban planning in the last few decades has been a growing recognition of the complex relationship between land use and transportation (see *Box 4. Energy and land use / transportation planning*). We understand much more than we did forty years ago about how building interstate highways or regional rail lines has enormous impacts on urban and suburban development. We also understand more about how the design of new developments determines what kinds of transportation can and cannot work there.

Following isolated experiments (some successful, some failed) with car-free zones, mall-like "festival" markets and new towns, a movement among architects and urban planners coalesced in the late 1980s and early 1990s to fundamentally challenge the car-dependence of modern urban and suburban development. Starting with concepts like pedestrian-oriented neighborhoods, "transit-oriented development," and human-scale vernacular architecture, this "New Urbanism" movement developed a vision of building pedestrian- and transit-friendly neighborhoods as an alternative to building conventional automobile-oriented suburbs of bedroom communities and malls.

One of the more widely-implemented versions of development related to this vision is often termed "smart growth," an approach that focuses on designing new transit-oriented urban and suburban areas with pedestrian amenities, higher residential densities, and "mixed use" development that allows, for example, apartments above ground-floor stores. The results of smart growth practices have been mixed, and the term has occasionally been misappropriated for real estate developments that do not fully adhere to smart growth principles. Still, the smart growth movement has helped change conventional planning with tools that help reduce the energy use and oil dependence of new communities. It's also prepared practicioners and communities for embracing more comprehensive planning and design practices that comprehensively consider how cities can meet their needs.

Smart Energy: Efficiency and alternative generation

The modern era that began after World War II seemed at first to be a new period of unlimited energy. The big hydroelectric dams begun in the 1930s were coming online, nuclear energy promised electricity "too cheap to meter," and the United States was churning out ever more oil as the world's largest oil producer. On top of all that, the largest oil fields in the world were just being discovered in the Middle East.

The vision of an unquestionably energy-rich future suddenly changed with the oil crises of the 1970s, the first of which immediately followed the 1971 peaking of U.S. oil production. Together with the growing awareness about pollution and other environmental issues, these oil crises spurred new and widespread interest in energy conservation, particularly for transportation and heating. This resulted in better fuel efficiency in cars and better thermal insulation for buildings, as well as new research into alternative energy technologies like photovoltaic cells and modern wind turbines. Energy conservation received renewed attention in the late 1980s and early 1990s as knowledge of global warming and the concept of "sustainable development" became more widespread.

Today, Europe and Japan lead the U.S. and Canada in overall energy efficiency, with significantly lower rates of personal energy consumption and more widespread use of energy-smart technologies like modern rail transit, "district heating" and green building. More and more U.S. and Canadian cities are pursuing sustainability-minded energy policies, however, adopting green building practices for public projects and diversifying their electricity sources with purchases of renewable power and "net metering" policies.

complex ecological systems that we do not fully understand. Therefore, management practices should assume that more will be learned about the resource over time, and polices may then need to change.

This concept of "planning for uncertainty" makes sense for managing any complex system—including cities. As described in a recent review of long-range sustainability planning tools prepared for the Vancouver, Canada region:

> *The [adaptive management] approach works well for urban planning, especially as planning time horizons extend and the complexity of urban areas starts to mimic natural systems.... [L]ong-term thinking is not about fixing in place a set of long-term policies; rather it is about adopting a process over the long-term that allows for frequent readjustment of current policy and plans in the face of new knowledge, new experience and new desires.* [35]

Consider a common problem for many North American cities: stormwater runoff. Many older North

American cities have combined sewer-stormwater systems that discharge a mix of stormwater and raw sewage into nearby waterways during heavy rains. Some cities are spending billions of dollars to fix this water pollution problem by building enormous new pipe systems to divert these extra overflows to treatment plants.

Planners using an adaptive management approach, however, would avoid committing all their resources to a single technological solution. They would recognize that there is a complex set of factors that can both mitigate and exacerbate the problem over time. Instead, they might address the problem through a variety of adjustable approaches: incentives for landowners to reduce impermeable surfaces on their property, programs to install "green roofs" and street runoff catchment swales (also known as "raingardens" or "bioswales"), and targeted sewer infrastructure upgrades.

The same thinking can be applied to energy and climate uncertainty. We don't know how energy supplies and prices will change over the coming decades, and we don't know what kind of local effects global warming will have. Therefore, we should pursue strategies that are conservative and iterative, closely monitor the results of new initiatives, and regularly re-assesses context and potential impacts.

I would say that most city planners are aware of our energy predicament. The biggest hurdle facing planners is that they're so swamped with the day-to-day workload... it's really hard for them to put aside enough time to devote to thinking about how they're going to handle new trends in city design.

I'm in a really lucky position right now. Our city is progressive-thinking, and our City Council is very supportive; they've given me some support and direction to work on [energy independence]... We have a very limited budget so they can't commit huge amounts of time and money, but they're not afraid to take a position on it.

– Alan Falleri, Director of Community Development, City of Willits, California

4. Responses to Energy and Climate Uncertainty

Now that we've established a basis for acting on energy and climate uncertainty, what do we do? Where do we begin?

This section will:

—review examples of what some U.S. and Canadian municipalities have already done in the last few years to address energy uncertainty, including case studies of three cities: Portland, Oregon; Hamilton, Ontario; and Willits, California; and,

—review some of the most significant local government approaches to climate uncertainty.

4.1 **Local government responses to energy uncertainty** Since oil prices started climbing beyond 15-year highs in 2004, cities of all sizes have begun addressing the challenges of peak oil (see Table 2). From targeted investments in local energy production to wide-ranging community vulnerability assessments, the responses of these jurisdictions recognize that peak oil and energy uncertainty pose serious threats to local social, economic and even environmental well-being.

Three case studies and four summaries of representative cities' actions are presented below to explore the variety of ways in which local governments are approaching these relatively new and little-understood problems. The Portland, Oregon metropolitan region is the subject of the lead case study, which considers the actions of both the city and the regional government as well as the larger context of community involvement and past planning decisions which helped shape these actions. The second case study looks at Hamilton, Ontario, a medium-sized city that solicited an external report on peak oil in the context of a controversial long-term economic development planning process. Rural Willits, California, is the third case study, providing an example of how city officials, staff and citizen volunteers can collaborate effectively to pursue both thorough and quick local responses to peak oil.

The summaries of peak oil responses in Burnaby (B.C.), Sebastopol (Calif.), Bloomington (Ind.), Austin (Tex.) and Spokane (Wash.) further highlight the wide range of responses that cities of different sizes and regions are pursuing. Following the case studies and summaries are some "lessons learned" from the successes and challenges of these experiences.

I think that the most important thing is to not panic because [energy uncertainty] is big... I think locally you just talk about everything and anything you can... you use your visibility as an elected official to advocate for sustainability, whether it's about increasing your recycling rates or getting the City fleet on biodiesel, or if you can talk local entrepreneurs into demonstration projects, or talking about how you spend your money for infrastructure. Just any chance you get, and hopefully something sticks, something works.

I don't know that there's a magic bullet for it. This is the fundamental—perhaps even defining—issue or series of issues over the next fifty years.

—Cliff Wood, City Council member, Providence, Rhode Island

Responses

The case studies and summaries presented here are limited to actions responding specifically to peak oil, and do not include all the various initiatives and policies these cities are pursuing to promote energy efficiency, renewable energy and other related goals.

Table 2:
Selected Local and Regional Government Responses to Peak Oil (U.S. & Canada)

Jurisdiction 2004 pop.	Actions
Southern California Association of Governments 17,797,500	Hosted Southern California Energy Conference 10 March 2006 on the global peaking of oil and natural gas production, mitigation measures and alternatives. Assessed regional energy demand and supply for 2007/08 comprehensive and transportation plans. www.scag.ca.gov/rcp/energy-summit.htm
Metro regional government, Portland, Oregon 1,374,486	Released policy white paper 18 April 2006, identifying "future oil supply uncertainty" as a timely risk management issue and establishing a basis for Metro to consider possible policy and program responses. www.metro-region.org/article.cfm?ArticleID=18951
San Francisco, California 744,230	First U.S. city to pass a peak oil resolution, 11 April 2006. Peak Oil Preparedness Task Force began meeting January 2008; scheduled to release final report in December 2008. www.postcarboncities.net/node/181
Austin, Texas 690,252	Passed resolution 7 June 2007 creating an Energy Depletion Risks Task Force to assess exposure to diminishing supplies of oil and natural gas and to make recommendations on addressing vulnerabilities. Task force started meeting on 4 September 2007. www.postcarboncities.net/node/233
Portland, Oregon 533,492	Passed resolution 10 May 2006 establishing a Peak Oil Task Force to study peak oil and its related consequences, seek community and business input, and develop recommendations on mitigation strategies. City Council accepted Task Force recommendations 7 March 2007. www.postcarboncities.net/node/206, www.portlandonline.com/osd/index.cfm?c=42894
Hamilton, Ontario 519,700	Received consultant report 13 April 2006 considering how future energy constraints might affect the City's roles as an energy user, public service provider and steward of community welfare. www.postcarboncities.net/node/267
Oakland, California 397,116	Passed resolution 17 October 2006 creating a Task Force "to develop an action plan for Oakland to become oil independent by 2020." The task force presented its final report in February 2008. www.postcarboncities.net/node/179, www.oaklandnet.com/oil
Spokane, Washington 199,400	Spokane became the first U.S. city to address climate change and peak oil together when it launched a sustainability strategic planning effort on 6 February 2008. A joint Task Force began its work in Spring. http://postcarboncities.net/node/2422
Burnaby, British Columbia 197,292	Released staff report 4 January 2006, concluding that "all levels of government and the corporate sector should begin preparations well before the peak [of global oil production]." www.postcarboncities.net/node/164
Bloomington, Indiana 69,320	Passed resolution 20 July 2006 acknowledging the challenge of peak oil, supporting adoption of a global depletion protocol, and urging federal and state action on peak oil and its consequences. The City Council created a Peak Oil Task Force in December 2007. www.postcarboncities.net/node/180
Westerley, Rhode Island 23,400	Passed resolution forming a peak oil task force on 17 March 2008.
Brattleboro, Vermont 8,290	Passed resolution forming a regional Peak Oil Task Force on 21 May 2007. http://www.postoilsolutions.org/peakoiltaskforce
Sebastopol, California 7,685	Held Town Hall meeting in Fall 2005, resulting in an ad hoc Energy Vulnerability Citizen's Committee to develop contingency plans for municipal services. Committee released final recommendations 3 April 2007. www.postcarboncities.net/node/134
Willits, California 5,098	Passed declaration supporting "sustainable localization." Worked with local citizen group to develop initiative for purchasing solar power for City buildings and water treatment facilities. http://willitseconomiclocalization.org/node/81
Franklin Town, New York 2,546	Passed resolution 6 December 2005 creating a Citizens' Commission to examine the issues raised by declining energy supplies and rising energy costs.

Metropolitan Region Case Study: Portland, Oregon

The Portland, Oregon case study includes both the City of Portland (population 534,000) and Metro, the regional government for the metropolitan area (population 1.4 million). Portland is one of only three large cities in the relatively sparsely populated Pacific Northwest.

Portland, Oregon is known throughout the United States as a model of foresighted urban development and sustainability-minded urban policy. From spearheading the movement against new urban highways in the 1970s to aggressively promoting green building and alternative fuels in this decade, Portland has long been a leader in pursuing compact, energy-efficient urban development through municipal initiatives supported by the private sector.

The Portland skyline as seen from the Multnomah County office building's eco-roof.

Background

Portland's recent responses to peak oil did not occur in a policy vacuum. They were part of a long-term trend at the city, regional and state levels to consider sustainability and livability goals in planning decisions:

- In the 1970s Portland became the first major U.S. city to demolish an existing urban highway, turning what had been a downtown waterfront freeway into a linear park. Later that decade, Portland made transportation planning history again when a movement of community members and planning advocates won the cancellation a federal city-to-suburb highway project, and reallocation of the project's funds to build one of the nation's first light rail transit lines.

- Also in the 1970s, the State of Oregon established a landmark set of land use planning laws that included the requirement to establish urban growth boundaries. In 1978 Portland area voters established an elected regional agency—now known as "Metro"—to coordinate land use planning, transportation planning, solid waste planning and other services.

- In the 1980s, Portland removed a central downtown parking garage to build a full-block public square, one of the first of a new generation of non-park urban spaces in the United States. By the early 1990s, a second major regional highway project was cancelled, due in part to an advocacy group's alternative proposal that incorporated farmland and air quality issues, and demonstrated the connection between land use and transportation.[36]

- In 1993 Portland became the first major U.S. city to adopt a strategy to reduce carbon dioxide emissions. In 1995, Metro established a 45-year regional growth concept focusing development on "centers and corridors" and protecting both farmland and recreation "greenspaces."

- In 2000, the City of Portland formed an Office of Sustainable Development (OSD) with responsibility for policies and programs on recycling, climate change, green building, food and energy. With a staff of over 40, OSD is now one of the largest such municipal offices in the country.

Growing Interest and Key Actions

Interest and concern about peak oil started growing noticeably in Portland in 2005 as the price of oil rose over $50 a barrel. Two public forums were instrumental in building awareness of peak oil among community leaders, business leaders, and regular citizens. A new citizen group, Portland Peak Oil[37], hosted public presentations and film screenings about peak oil and its possible ramifications, and began organizing to encourage government

Every time we get a spike in gas prices, people start to think about energy. Our job is to be thinking long-term for people, kind of like the retirement planner, coming up with a situation analysis on the issue of energy.

- Councilmember Rex Burkholder, Metro, Portland, Oregon

Responses

> One of the issues that we keep running into is, *oil is economy.*
>
> - Rowan Wolf, sociology professor, Portland Peak Oil Task Force

action. In early 2006, the locally-popular Illahee lecture series focused a whole season on oil and water issues, bringing in prominent peak oil thinkers like James Howard Kunstler and Kenneth Deffeyes, and concluding with a symposium aimed at regional business and government leaders.

Also at this time, Metro[38] Councilmember Rex Burkholder—inspired from attending the November 2005 World Oil Forum hosted by Denver Mayor John Hickenlooper—commissioned an internal policy analysis on peak oil and what it might mean for Metro's planning and public service responsibilities. The resulting policy white paper (written by the author of this Guidebook while a policy associate at Metro) characterized the problem as "future oil supply uncertainty" and established a basis for the Metro Council to consider possible policy and program responses. The Council's acceptance of the white paper received favorable front-page coverage in Portland's daily business newspaper, spurring wider awareness of the issue.

The Portland Peak Oil Task Force

While the Metro white paper was in development, members of Portland Peak Oil developed a draft City Council resolution calling on the City to officially address peak oil. Portland Peak Oil then worked with City Commissioner Dan Saltzman and his staff to finalize the resolution and bring it to a vote; it passed unanimously in May 2006.

The Portland resolution was particularly significant because it established a broad-based Task Force of appointed citizens who were charged with community input and developing recommendations. The specific charges of the Task Force were:

a. To acquire and study current and credible data and information on the issues of peak oil and natural gas production and the related economic and other societal consequences;

b. To seek community and business input on the impacts and proposed solutions;

c. To develop recommendations to City Council in this calendar year on strategies the City and its bureaus can take to mitigate the impacts of declining energy supplies in areas including, but not limited to: transportation, business and home energy use, water, food security, health care, communications, land use planning, and wastewater treatment. These recommendations will be considered as amendments to the Local Action Plan on Global Warming when it is revised in 2007 and integrated into city-wide long term strategic planning; and

d. To propose methods of educating the public about this issue in order to create positive behavior change among businesses and residents that reduce dependence on fossil fuels.[39]

The Task Force began meeting in July 2006; its members included citizens with a broad range of professional backgrounds:

—a project director for an energy consulting firm,
—an advertising executive with a local radio station,
—a retired farmer,
—an architect and planning commission member,
—the former chief of staff to the mayor during the 1970s energy crisis,
—an attorney for the regional government,
—the Executive Director of a local non-profit organization,
—a sociology professor,
—a public health educator, and
—a representative from Portland Peak Oil.

City staff, including a representative from the Oregon Department of Energy, prepared a briefing book for the Task Force that included background information on global oil production, facts and statistics on regional fuel delivery, and existing local plans and policies related to transportation, food, housing and buildings.

For the initial meeting, City staff prepared suggestions for organizing the research. They also clarified the Task Force's mission as a "narrowing exercise" focused on exploring the ways in which the ramifications of peak oil might affect Portland, and on developing specific strategies to mitigate those impacts.

With little precedent to guide them on this complex undertaking, Task Force members faced a challenge in deciding how to structure their approach. The Task Force broke up into four sub-groups, each focusing on a different sector: Land Use and Transportation; Food and Agriculture; Public Services; and Economic Change. Task Force staff encouraged members to "keep the discussion at a high altitude," to focus on identifying impacts first before talking about recommendations, and to be concrete in their discussions. The sub-groups collected information through group and personal research, interviewing key stakeholders (e.g., the Chief Financial Officer of a major supermarket chain) and inviting issue experts to present at meetings (e.g., City transportation planning staff).

Interestingly, each Task Force sub-group developed its own process for best determining impacts and vulnerabilities. For example, the Land Use and Transportation Group took a risk analysis approach by listing items under a few major categories ("Freight and Fuel," "People Transportation" and "Land Use") and then placing them within a matrix by impact and probability. In contrast, the Food and Agriculture group listed impacts under a greater diversity of categories, identifying both first tier impacts (e.g., "Higher fuel costs for transport to and from processing plants.") and second tier impacts (e.g., "Change in number and location of processing plants.").

On 7 March 2007, the City Council accepted the Task Force's final report and recommendations, which are summarized in *Box 7* (page 43). The top recommendation—to reduce total oil and natural gas consumption by 50 percent over the next 25 years—was derived in part from the Oil Depletion Protocol target of a 2.6% reduction of oil consumption per year.[40] According to City staff, the Task Force recommendations now form a key stream of input into an upcoming three-year overhaul of the City's Comprehensive Plan, and will likely be integrated into a late 2007 revision of the city/county climate protection plan.[41]

Observations

The efforts of both Metro and the City of Portland owed much to the relationships and collaboration across key organizations:

- The citizen group Portland Peak Oil played a significant role in the drafting and enacting of the City resolution establishing a Peak Oil Task Force.
- The Peak Oil Task Force was made up of volunteers from other agencies, organizations and the community.
- Metro had resources available to pursue the initial study thanks to Portland State University providing a graduate student (the author) to the Metro Council as part-time policy staff.
- Periodic communication between people at Portland Peak Oil, the City, Metro and Illahee (the non-profit that organized a lecture series and regional leaders' symposium on peak oil) facilitated collaboration and information-sharing.

Also, the Portland area already has a strong regional planning and policy-making framework through which it can choose address energy and climate uncertainty issues (indeed, Metro has already started to integrate the issue of energy supply uncertainty into the Regional Transportation Plan, for which it is responsible).

Metro Regional Government

IMPETUS: Elected official's interest.

ACTION: Produced an internal policy paper on "oil supply uncertainty".

RESULTS: Peak oil considerations are being integrated into planning activities.

City Of Portland

IMPETUS: Citizen group proposal; elected official's interest.

ACTION: Passed resolution recognizing peak oil and establishing a Task Force to develop response recommendations.

RESULTS: Task Force recommendations are expected to be integrated with City policy and programs.

For its preliminary impacts report, the Food & Agriculture sub-group of the Portland Peak Oil Task Force developed six scoping areas and twenty-eight questions to guide their next steps.

It's a mix of useful and useless questions right now, but the point, perhaps, is to be exhaustive in hopes of getting the really good ones —and their answers—that may prove very useful later on, and that may spur different and better questions

- Food & Agriculture Sub-Group member, Portland Peak Oil Task Force

Responses

Resources

—The Metro white paper, "Future Oil Supply Uncertainty and Metro":
http://www.metro-region.org/article.cfm?ArticleID=18951

—The Portland Peak Oil Task Force final report, resolution and other materials are available from the City of Portland's Office of Sustainable Development:
http://www.portlandonline.com/osd/index.cfm?c=ecije

—The Portland Peak Oil grassroots group continues to advocate for further City action on peak oil. Their website includes additional resources and discussion:
http://www.portlandpeakoil.org/

—Post Carbon Institute maintains a page on Portland's peak oil actions, including all the Task Force documents as well as links to follow-up articles and presentations.
http://postcarboncities.net/portland_or

Box 7   Portland (Ore.) Peak Oil Task Force Recommendations

Excerpted from the Portland Peak Oil Task Force's final report, "Descending the Oil Peak: Navigating the Transition from Oil and Natural Gas." These recommendations were adopted by the Portland City Council on 7 March 2007. Available online at http://postcarboncities.net/portland_or.

While all the recommendations are important, **achieving a significant reduction in oil and natural gas use** is a necessity for easing the transition to an energy-constrained future.

    1. Reduce total oil and natural gas consumption by 50 percent over the next 25 years.

Leadership builds the public will, community spirit and institutional capacity needed to implement the ambitious changes. Leadership is needed to build partnerships to address these issues at a regional and statewide level.

    2. Inform citizens about peak oil and foster community and community-based solutions.

    3. Engage business, government and community leaders to initiate planning and policy change.

Urban design addresses the challenge at a community scale.

    4. Support land use patterns that reduce transportation needs, promote walkability and provide easy access to services and transportation options.

    5. Design infrastructure to promote transportation options and facilitate efficient movement of freight, and prevent infrastructure investments that would not be prudent given fuel shortages and higher prices.

Expanded efficiency and conservation programs shape the many energy choices made by individual households and businesses.

    6. Encourage energy-efficient and renewable transportation choices.

    7. Expand building energy-efficiency programs and incentives for all new and existing structures.

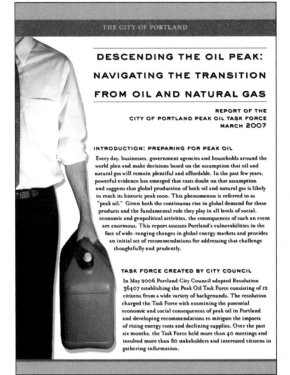

THE CITY OF PORTLAND

DESCENDING THE OIL PEAK: NAVIGATING THE TRANSITION FROM OIL AND NATURAL GAS

REPORT OF THE
CITY OF PORTLAND PEAK OIL TASK FORCE
MARCH 2007

INTRODUCTION: PREPARING FOR PEAK OIL

Every day, businesses, government agencies and households around the world plan and make decisions based on the assumption that oil and natural gas will remain plentiful and affordable. In the past few years, powerful evidence has emerged that casts doubt on that assumption and suggests that global production of both oil and natural gas is likely to reach its historic peak soon. This phenomenon is referred to as "peak oil." Given both the continuous rise in global demand for these products and the fundamental role they play in all levels of social, economic and geopolitical activities, the consequences of such an event are enormous. This report assesses Portland's vulnerabilities in the face of wide-ranging changes in global energy markets and provides an initial set of recommendations for addressing that challenge thoughtfully and prudently.

TASK FORCE CREATED BY CITY COUNCIL

In May 2006 Portland City Council adopted Resolution 36407 establishing the Peak Oil Task Force consisting of 12 citizens from a wide variety of backgrounds. The resolution charged the Task Force with examining the potential economic and social consequences of peak oil in Portland and developing recommendations to mitigate the impacts of rising energy costs and declining supplies. Over the past six months, the Task Force held more than 40 meetings and involved more than 80 stakeholders and interested citizens in gathering information.

Sustainable economic development fosters the growth of businesses that can supply energy efficient solutions and provide employment and wealth creation in a new economic context.

    8. Preserve farmland and expand local food production and processing.

    9. Identify and promote sustainable business opportunities.

Social and economic support systems will be needed to help Portlanders dislocated by the effects of fuel price increases.

    10. Redesign the safety net and protect vulnerable and marginalized populations.

Emergency plans should be in place to respond to sudden price increases or supply interruptions.

    11. Prepare emergency plans for sudden and severe shortages.

Responses

Medium-sized City Case Study: Hamilton, Ontario

Hamilton, Ontario (population 519,700) lies in southern Ontario, on the edge of the Toronto metropolitan region and roughly equidistant from both central Toronto and Buffalo, New York. The ninth largest city in Canada, Hamilton has been addressing energy and air quality issues through a variety of initiatives since the oil crises of the 1970s. These have included promoting neighborhood designs optimized for passive solar heating and purchasing "green" vehicles for its municipal fleet.

Hamilton, Ontario

In 2003 Hamilton began developing a 30-year growth management strategy, a key component of which was an "aerotropolis" airport-centric economic development concept,[42] in which Hamilton would become a transportation and business hub centered on an expanded airport and associated growth in both freight and passenger flights. The aerotropolis plan ran into opposition in 2005, with some citizens and City Councilors resisting a related expansion of the city's urban growth boundary, and calling for peak oil and future energy constraints to be considered in the 30-year strategy.[43] Spurred by this opposition, the City Council commissioned a report by transportation consultant and former Toronto City Councilor Richard Gilbert to consider how future energy constraints might affect Hamilton's long-term planning strategy. A citizen group, Hamiltonians for Progressive Development, was also formed to maintain pressure on the aerotropolis and energy issues.

Gilbert's final report, entitled "Hamilton: The Electric City," assessed how the City might best address future energy constraints in view of its roles as an energy user, public service provider, and sustainer of the community's overall welfare. It included these points:

- Notes that a peak oil strategy must deal with both existing buildings and transportation choices.

- Calls on the City to pay more attention to energy issues in its strategic planning, and to redevelop the 30-year growth management strategy with energy as the guiding principle.

- Outlines four quantitative targets for community-wide energy use and production to be considered in the planning of transport, land use and economic development.

- Discusses specific concepts and opportunities for meeting energy targets in transportation, land use, building, new energy production, and economic and social development.

- Addresses specific issues raised by City Council, including the aerotropolis project, goods movement, the City vehicle fleet and local rail transit.

Upon Gilbert's presentation of the final report in April 2006, the City Council passed a resolution specifying follow-up reports from City staff, including as regards:

- the feasibility of the report's recommendations on reducing energy use by two-thirds by 2018,

- the feasibility of using electricity to run trolley buses and Bus Rapid Transit routes,

- policy to encourage green building certification for all new construction,

- the feasibility of establishing an Energy Cluster as part of the City's economic development strategy,

- the feasibility of preparing a local business park as an "Eco-Park" sharing energy and reusing waste materials among different industrial tenants.

> **[A] fairly significant portion of our urban fabric and built form is already committed to: it's under development or currently exists. That has a lot of implications because a lot of homeowners will be impacted by rising energy costs, and part of the city's response must recognize and deal with that.**
>
> – Stephen Robichaud, Manager, Growth Management, City of Hamilton

The process surrounding the report and its recommendations has been somewhat contentious, with Hamiltonians for Progressive Development protesting that the City was taking too long to produce the follow-up report, and City Councilor David Braden charging that the City had obstructed the report's development because an examination of future energy costs would reflect unfavorably on the aerotropolis project.[44]

According to City staff the report has been helpful in bringing existing sustainability efforts—including the creation of an Office of Energy Initiatives, the purchase of fuel-efficient vehicles for the City fleet, and consideration of a private initiative to install micro wind turbines on municipal buildings—under the same "conceptual umbrella." The report is also expected to influence long-term budgeting and strategic planning.[45]

Observations

IMPETUS: Efforts of local citizen group and personal interest of certain elected officials responding to both general energy concerns and a specific City-favored economic development strategy.

ACTION: City Council commissioned an external report to assess how future energy constraints might affect long-range planning and development.

RESULTS: Little immediate follow-up on the report, although it has contributed to a conceptual framework for long-term energy-related policy and programmatic initiatives.

Resources

—Richard Gilbert's "Hamilton: The Electric City" report:
   http://www.postcarboncities.net/node/267

—Full transcript of City Council's discussion of the "Electric City" report:
   http://www.hamiltoncatch.org/archives/cow/cow_060428a.htm

—Hamilton's 30-year growth strategy:
   Search for "GRIDS" on http://www.myhamilton.ca

—Hamiltonians for Progressive Development:
   http://www.progressivedevelopment.ca

Responses

> As an elected official, I had to be very interested and concerned with the financial aspects of the project to make sure that it paid for us to do this. Being environmental and keeping the Earth clean is OK, but it still needs to make financial sense.
>
> The way it's working out, if we can offset all of our electric bill for that facility, hopefully that amount of money that we normally send to PG&E would be used instead to pay off the loan. So in essence it's not costing the City any money to put the solar panels in... And then of course when the loan is paid, our electricity is virtually free.
>
> – Councilmember Ron Orenstein, City of Willits, California

Smaller City Case Study: Willits, California

Willits, California (population 5,098) is a rural Northern California town, 135 miles north of San Francisco. Known as the "Gateway to the Redwoods," Willits initiated some of the first city efforts in the U.S. related specifically to peak oil.

The impetus for action in Willits came from a local grassroots group, WELL ("Willits Economic LocaLization")[46], which included City Councilmember Ron Orenstein among its members. In early 2005, WELL conducted an inventory of the community's energy usage, including fuel sources, costs per person and greenhouse gas emissions. Among the conclusions of the inventory were that cooperative ownership of the electric utility might reduce prices for the community, and that wood had potential as a local energy source.

According to Brian Corzilius, lead author of WELL's energy inventory, some of the more important findings of Willits' assessment effort came from "just starting to talk to people in the city and community."[47] For example the energy inventory committee members discovered that the local hospital takes its water from an outflow halfway down the City water tank, and that should the water supply fall below that level the fire department was responsible for providing fresh water. Knowing that the water tank was dependent on electric pumps to stay full, and that the largest portion of Willits' electricity (33%) was produced by gas-fired turbines, the committee realized it had uncovered a potentially serious vulnerability in basic services that, at first glance, didn't seem to relate to oil or natural gas at all.

Following publication of the energy inventory, Councilmember Orenstein led City Council in establishing an ad hoc energy committee to further consider municipal options for using alternative energy sources. The committee reviewed all municipal electricity expenses for a year, and developed suggestions for powering City facilities with solar power. By late 2006, the City had used this information to acquire around $1 million in grants to install a solar energy system to power the water treatment plant and sell excess electricity back to the electric utility. This initiative alone will eliminate 30% of the City's electricity bill, paying for itself in a matter of years.

Unlike the Portland Peak Oil Task Force, which had easy access to energy baseline data thanks to the early personal involvement of two State Department of Energy staff, the Willits group had to seek out its own data on energy usage, fuel delivery and state energy policy, and develop analyses of this data from scratch. Some of their initial analyses focused on determining how much community money was leaving the area to pay for energy; for the greater Willits community of 13,000, they determined this figure to be $30 million, half of which was for transportation fuel. With these data, they were able to make a compelling case for efforts to stimulate local businesses (in hopes of creating new local jobs, and thus reducing the need for residents to commute out-of-town for work) and to boost local tax revenues. They also used this to tie their efforts to local issues such as the need for good local jobs.

The City of Willits joined ICLEI's Cities for Climate Protection Program in August 2006 (see *Box 9*, page 53).

Observations

IMPETUS: Report submitted by an citizen group (of which an elected municipal official was a member).

ACTION: The City established an ad hoc committee to consider municipal energy initiatives.

RESULTS: The City pursued at least one of the recommended initiatives.

Resources

—The Energy Committee's report, as well as other documents from WELL such as a description of how they conducted their energy inventory, are available at: http://willitseconomiclocalization.org/node/81

Summary of other cities' actions

A number of other cities have taken action with regard to peak oil in the last few years. Here's a quick look at what happened in some of these jurisdictions:

Burnaby, British Columbia

Stuart Ramsey, Transportation Planner for the City of Burnaby, British Columbia, learned about peak oil in 2004 and began talking about it with colleagues and elected officials. After a screening of the film "The End of Suburbia" caught the attention of the Mayor and the Chair of Burnaby's Transportation Committee, the Committee requested a staff report on the issue.

The resulting 17-page report, released in January 2006, focused on the municipal ramifications of a global peak in oil production, the data supporting peak oil, the debate surrounding peak oil, and general energy supply impacts that will likely be associated with peaking. The report also included general ideas for addressing impacts on transportation and heating from the municipal government's role as both a government agency and a corporate citizen.

The report has raised awareness about energy supply issues internally and has been used to provide background on certain City Council decisions, such as the promotion of cycling infrastructure or opposition to freeway widening. It has also helped further discussion of energy issues in the regional government of the Vancouver metropolitan area (the offices of which are located in Burnaby).

The Transportation Committee report is available online at http://www.postcarboncities.net/node/164.

> *Since our report, 'peak oil' has entered our lexicon and comes up regularly in staff discussions. We also include it in other reports to Council—for example, in favor of cycling infrastructure, or against freeway widening—since the original report provided the background.*
>
> *- Stuart Ramsey, Transportation Planner, City of Burnaby, British Columbia*

Sebastopol, California

Spurred by the interest of Mayor Larry Robinson, in September 2005 the City of Sebastopol sponsored a Town Hall meeting on "future energy needs and the economic and social consequences of a potential sharp increase in oil and gas prices." The meeting led to the Council establishing an ad hoc Energy Vulnerability Citizens Committee including local business leaders, journalists and other citizens. The committee was charged with analyzing community vulnerabilities and developing contingency plans for providing primary (public safety, water) and secondary (transportation, schools) municipal services in various energy-constrained scenarios.

The committee released its final report in April 2007 (see *Box 8*); it is available online at http://www.postcarboncities.net/node/134.

> *Given the failure of the federal government to adequately address either global warming or America's energy vulnerability, it is up to local governments, small businesses and citizens groups to take the lead. While we can't know with any great certainty how these two world changing events will impact us, the longer we wait to develop contingency plans, the more vulnerable we will be. Sebastopol is committed to doing whatever we can to prepare for the coming crisis.*
>
> *- Former Mayor Larry Robinson, Sebastopol, California*

Box 8 Sebastopol (Calif.) Citizens Advisory Group on Energy Vulnerability Recommendations

Excerpted from "Charting a Path for a New Energy Future for Sebastopol," Sebastopol (California) Citizens Advisory Group on Energy Vulnerability, 3 April 2007; available online at http://postcarboncities.net/node/134.

To serve the City, we have identified key actions that the City can do in this regard. Below is a summary of our recommendations; the body of this report describes our underlying analysis and important specifics about implementation.

First Steps

• Develop and pass an Energy Transition Resolution.
• Appoint the City Council Energy and Sustainable Practices Subcommittee to implement this resolution and track the progress of these recommendations through the City Council process.
• Establish a standing Citizens' Technical Advisory Committee (CTAC) to assist the City in implementing this resolution and these recommendations.
• Direct City departments to determine departmental vulnerabilities and propose implementation plans for this resolution, which the City Council Energy Subcommittee will then evaluate and prioritize, with CTAC's assistance.
• Explore potential partnerships and alliances with other organizations and government entities to share information and collaborate on accomplishing, and sharing the costs, of these activities.

Implementation Steps

• Develop procedures for easily tracking City energy use and costs, and reporting these annually to the City Council, to observe trends and adjust actions and priorities.
• Seek permission to aggregate the City's electrical loads, to apply credits from solar panels to other City locations.
• Continue reducing City usage of fossil fuels and electricity, even in situations where costs can be passed through to users...
• Proactively invest in additional energy technologies that transition away from fossil fuels. To do this, explore creative funding mechanisms and the use of other alternative energy sources, such as wind and solar thermal...
• Prepare for longer-term outages and emergencies. To do this, prepare plans for more drastic energy-limited situations, including determining the basic electrical consumption level needed for each department, how long current backup options would last, if this should be increased for longer outages, and other backup technology that might be useful...

• Plan future City revenues in the face of these dynamics. To do this, add energy vulnerability scenarios to the current revenue development planning process and to area "Buy Local" campaigns...
• Reduce risks of impacts on employee availability by assessing how sustained and serious fuel shortages or price increases might impact the availability of commuting employees and establishing incentives to use alternatives to single occupancy vehicles.
• Reduce risks from trash collection cost increases and pickup failures, by encouraging WMI's use of non-fossil fuel and reducing the City's total trash amount, with the goal of becoming a Zero Waste city.

Making Broader Connections

Because the City's activities are interdependent with those of the community and other levels of government, it is vital that the City also keep an eye on the larger community picture as it evolves—both to consider how this could impact the City's ability to maintain appropriate levels of service, and to explore how the City can constructively influence activities in other spheres. Larger potential impacts of these dynamics include harm to transportation systems, food supplies, other government entities, and the overall economy. The ripple effects of these unprecedented challenges and events will require both anticipation and flexibility in response.

To support constructive proactive action in the larger community, we advise the City to:
• Establish a Community Outreach Committee to make recommendations to the greater Sebastopol community about appropriate measures which could be taken to adapt to future uncertainties regarding energy supplies.
• Identify ways that the City can encourage actions at other levels of government to reduce energy use and transition away from fossil fuel energy sources.
• Consider joining with other cities to implement Community Choice Aggregation (CCA), in order to buy and support local green power. In the future, consider becoming a municipal utility, to better access local energy sources and control rates.
• Expand citizen conservation and adoption of alternatives. Educate users on the energy component in the costs of City services, including water, sewer, etc.

Bloomington, Indiana

Following years of interest in sustainability issues including peak oil, Councilmember Dave Rollo spearheaded creation of the Bloomington Commission on Sustainability in May 2005. Rollo built community support for taking municipal action on peak oil by making presentations at community meetings (including the Chamber of Commerce), and bringing *Powerdown* author Richard Heinberg to speak in September of that year. In July 2006, Bloomington City Council passed a resolution recognizing that the City "must prepare for the inevitability of oil peak," supporting adoption of the Oil Depletion Protocol[48], and urging state and federal officials to prepare for the consequences of a peak in global oil production. In December 2007, the City Council passed a resolution creating a Peak Oil Task Force to explore the community's vulnerability to energy decline and crisis, and to make recommendations to the Council and Mayor.

> *It's hard to stop the inertia of the way we've been doing things in the past. Developers still want to develop 3,000 and 5,000 square foot homes with natural gas. This is the wrong way to go. At the City we're trying to do as much as we can to encourage sustainability, but there's still an inertia in what we do that's pointed totally in the wrong direction.*

> *The turning of the ship is going to take a while. I think we have to work at all societal levels.*

> *- City Councilor Dave Rollo, Bloomington, Indiana*

Austin, Texas

In June 2007 the Austin City Council passed a resolution creating an Energy Depletion Risks Task Force to assess the City's exposure to potentially diminishing supplies of oil and natural gas and to make recommendations for addressing any perceived vulnerabilities. The Task Force is specifically tasked with developing a comprehensive risk assessment and contingency plan. Part of its charge includes seeking community and business input, as well as coordinating with higher-level agencies to gather information on issues related to the planning uncertainties and the economic impacts of declining energy supplies.

The resolution followed nearly a year of organizing by both the citizen group Austin Crude Awakening and key staff and officials at the City of Austin; the effort was led by Roger Duncan, former City Councilman and current General Manager of Austin's community-owned electric utility. The Task Force started meeting in September 2007, its membership including Duncan and representatives of various City departments, the regional natural gas utility, the regional transportation authority, a regional sustainability leadership coalition, the University of Texas, and Austin Crude Awakening. The Task Force is following the model of the Portland Peak Oil Task Force by interviewing subject matter experts in four specific issue areas: land use and transportation; food and agriculture; public and social services; and economic change.

> *The availability of oil and gas to Austin is not only critical to our economy, but essential to the health and safety of our community. I cannot think of a more important issue that needs to be addressed by Austin.*

> *- Roger Duncan, General Manager, Austin Energy*

Spokane, Washington

Spokane, the second-largest city in the state of Washington, became the first U.S. city to address climate change and peak oil together when it launched a sustainability strategic planning effort in February 2008. The City received a state grant to fund the effort, which is meant to find solutions to the sustainability challenges arising from global warming and the changing global energy situation. The resulting strategic action plan will address the ways that future climate and energy uncertainties may impact the city government's operations, services, programs and policies.

A mayor-appointed citizen task force leads the strategic planning effort, supported by work groups and technical assistance from city staff and other experts. Members include

Responses

representatives from the local and state governments, universities, the home builders association, the transit agency, the local energy company and other private and non-profit sector stakeholders. It will set out strategies for the city government to reduce its operational costs, ensure its ability to serve taxpayers, and support residents' and businesses' efforts to also address these trends. A draft plan is due for release by February 2009.

By aggressively pursuing strategies now that prepare us for future energy and climate uncertainties, Spokane will manage challenges while increasing our competitive advantage over other cities. It just makes sense.

- Spokane Mayor Mary Verner

Lessons Learned

The local government initiatives discussed above differ widely in intent, scope, and organization. From city to city, elected officials and agency staff showed varying degrees of leadership and engagement; in almost all instances, however, citizen initiatives[49] played decisive roles in spurring local governments to prepare studies, set up task forces, and make official statements.

Overall a few key lessons can be drawn from these cities' experiences:

- **Make a clear government statement on the issue:**
Not all local governments that have considered energy uncertainty have gone on to assess their vulnerabilities. Nevertheless, a clear government statement—whether a Council resolution or a policy white paper—opens opportunities for both staff and the community to discuss the issue and engage with it later on.

- **Engage the issue with both government and the community:**
The efforts in Portland, Willits, Sebastopol all were able to address a broad swath of issues thanks to volunteer citizen involvement. A volunteer citizen commission can bring valuable resources and help establish community buy-in, especially if some members are drawn from the business community and other government agencies. Municipal staff in turn provide the consistency and guidance that is essential for such a complex undertaking. Smaller cities that can't afford extra staff time should consider using an elected official or volunteer retired staff for such roles.

- **Organize and lead task forces carefully:**
An interview and referral process helped ensure that the Portland Peak Oil Task Force was made up of people who knew their fields and knew how to work effectively in a collaborative group process. The Task Force also benefited greatly from having a few City staff on hand to assist the process and assemble technical data, allowing members to concentrate on interviewing experts, researching impacts and digesting information.

On the other hand, volunteers and staff on some municipal task forces (including one not covered in the case studies) reported challenges such as insufficient timeframes, lack of clear direction, and disruptive volunteers. While the organization and execution of any special inquiry should be done with care, municipalities should be especially mindful when undertaking volunteer-staffed inquiries to ensure that everyone's time is well spent.

See *Section 5.3 What your city can do* for a summary of our recommendations for local government action, based in part on these cities' experiences. Then see *Appendix: Making a government statement on peak oil* and *Appendix: Establishing a peak oil task force* for suggestions on taking action in your own jurisdiction.

4.2 Local government responses to climate uncertainty

At the 1992 "Earth Summit" on sustainable development in Rio de Janeiro, the world's governments agreed that global warming posed serious risks to humanity. They launched two key efforts to organize the international response: the United Nations Framework Convention on Climate Change (UNFCCC), which led to the Kyoto Protocol, and the Agenda 21 program, which called for both global and local action on sustainable development. Initial governmental efforts generally focused on mitigating greenhouse gas emissions, especially in industrialized countries. With the release of the third series of Intergovernmental Panel on Climate Change (IPCC) reports in 2001, however, many governments began to focus more attention on adapting to those effects of climate change that could not be avoided.

The United States has largely remained an outsider to international efforts on climate change. The federal government has steadfastly refused to ratify the Kyoto Protocol since signing it in 1997, and under the Bush Administration it has repeatedly interfered with and even censored government scientific reporting on global warming.[50] At the state and local levels, few governments paid more than scant attention to either mitigation or adaptation until quite recently. Canadian governments at all levels have generally been more responsive to climate change, although in 2006 the federal government backpedaled on its commitments to the Kyoto Protocol, which it ratified in 2002.

There are two broad ways that local governments are responding to climate change:

- Mitigation efforts focus on systematically reducing greenhouse gas emissions through initiatives related to energy efficiency and renewable energy. Most serious local mitigation efforts attempt to reduce greenhouse gas emissions at or below the levels called for in the Kyoto Protocol.

- Adaptation efforts are significantly more complex to pursue because the local environmental and economic impacts of climate change are difficult to predict, as are the feedback effects of those impacts at larger scales. Effective adaptation requires a comprehensive assessment of localized risks, and an integration of climate change considerations into all areas of decision-making.

In this guidebook we have characterized the global warming problem for local governments as "climate uncertainty." This is meant to reflect the uncertainty about how exactly climate change will affect local environments and economies, as well as the uncertainty about how greenhouse gas reduction efforts actually affect climate change.

Now let's take a look at how local governments can respond to climate uncertainty through both mitigation and adaptation.

The devastation wrought by Hurricane Katrina in September 2005 has come to symbolize both the changing risks that global warming poses for cities and the need for local governments to prepare for those risks, with or without federal help.

Other countries have done far more to get ready for the effects of global warming than the United States...[I]n the United States, climate experts say, without federal direction it can be difficult for local governments to respond. Many have never planned 100 years into the future. And officials may have more immediate priorities or lack the expertise to know how to prepare.

'People are overwhelmed, they don't have a legal mandate or resources to deal with it,' said Susanne Moser, a geographer at the National Center for Atmospheric Research in Colorado and a contributing author to [the April 2007 IPCC report]. 'But we need to.'

- "US lags on plans for climate change," by Beth Daley, Boston Globe, 5 April 2007.

Responses

Mitigation

In 1993, one year after the Rio Earth Summit, the International Council for Local Environmental Initiatives (ICLEI) launched the Cities for Climate Protection Campaign[51] to support local governments in greenhouse gas emissions monitoring and reduction. This program is the most widely-used method to date that local governments have adopted to address global warming. Cities for Climate Protection leads participants through a five-milestone framework (see *Box 9*) to reduce emissions through policies and practices that conserve energy and develop renewable energy sources. As of 2008, more than 1,000 local governments worldwide were participating in this campaign, including over 500 in the U.S. and Canada.

On February 16, 2005 the Kyoto Protocol went into effect for the 141 countries that ratified it, which notably did not include the United States and Australia. Since then, four significant efforts have been launched to promote and support local government action on climate change:

- **U.S. Mayors Climate Protection Agreement**
  On the same day that the Kyoto Protocol went into effect, Seattle Mayor Greg Nickels issued a challenge for U.S. mayors to agree to "meet or beat" the greenhouse gas reduction goals of the Protocol in their own cities. This challenge was formalized as the U.S. Mayors Climate Protection Agreement (see *Box 10*) and adopted unanimously by the U.S. Conference of Mayors in June 2005. As of 2008, over 800 mayors had signed the Agreement, representing all 50 states as well as the ten largest cities.

- **World Mayors and Municipal Leaders Declaration on Climate Change**
  At the December 2005 United Nations Climate Change Conference (which included the eleventh meeting of nations party to the UNFCCC and the first meeting of those party to the Kyoto Protocol) the parallel Fourth Municipal Leaders Summit on Climate Change adopted the World Mayors and Municipal Leaders Declaration on Climate Change. The Declaration endorsed emissions reduction targets of 30% by 2020 and 80% by 2050 for developed countries, and asserted the need for local governments to have a greater role in UNFCCC efforts.

- **Clinton Climate Initiative**
  In August 2006, the William J. Clinton Foundation launched a partnership with the Large Cities Climate Leadership Group by establishing the Clinton Climate Initiative. The Initiative is organizing an international purchasing consortium of the world's largest cities to bring down the cost of energy-efficient products and to accelerate development of emissions-reducing technologies. Although formal membership in the program is restricted to the world's 40 largest cities, smaller cities can receive some benefit by joining as affiliates.

- **Cool Counties Climate Stabilization Declaration**
  On 16 July 2007, twelve large U.S. counties and the Sierra Club launched the Cool Counties Climate Stabilization Declaration, in which signatories pledge to reduce global warming emissions 80 percent by 2050. The Declaration also calls for vehicle fuel economy standards to be raised to 35 miles per gallon within a decade.

The U.S. Conference of Mayors, ICLEI, the City of Seattle and the Sundance Institute have partnered to make global warming information and mitigation resources—including handbooks and best practices reports—available at a single online portal, www.coolmayors.com. The U.S. and Canadian affiliates of the international Climate Action Network[52] include organizations that are working on global warming at the local, state/provincial, regional and national levels. Other efforts are underway at state and regional levels such as the development of carbon "cap-and-trade" systems, renewable portfolio standards, emissions targets and climate action plans.[53]

Box 9   ICLEI's Cities for Climate Protection Campaign

From the ICLEI website, www.iclei.org.

Local governments join the Cities for Climate Protection (CCP) campaign by passing a resolution pledging to reduce greenhouse gas emissions from their local government operations and throughout their communities. ICLEI then assists the cities to undertake the CCP's five milestones.

The five milestones of the CCP and the methodology that underlies the milestones provide a simple, standardized means of calculating greenhouse gas emissions, of establishing targets to lower emissions, of reducing greenhouse gas emissions and of monitoring, measuring and reporting performance.

The five milestones are:

Milestone 1. Conduct a baseline emissions inventory and forecast. Based on energy consumption and waste generation, the city calculates greenhouse gas emissions for a base year (e.g., 2000) and for a forecast year (e.g., 2015). The inventory and forecast provide a benchmark against which the city can measure progress.

Milestone 2. Adopt an emissions reduction target for the forecast year. The city establishes an emission reduction target for the city. The target both fosters political will and creates a framework to guide the planning and implementation of measures.

Milestone 3. Develop a Local Action Plan. Through a multi-stakeholder process, the city develops a Local Action Plan that describes the policies and measures that the local government will take to reduce greenhouse gas emissions and achieve its emissions reduction target. Most plans include a timeline, a description of financing mechanisms, and an assignment of responsibility to departments and staff. In addition to direct greenhouse gas reduction measures, most plans also incorporate public awareness and education efforts.

Milestone 4. Implement policies and measures. The city implements the policies and measures contained in their Local Action Plan. Typical policies and measures implemented by CCP participants include energy efficiency improvements to municipal buildings and water treatment facilities, streetlight retrofits, public transit improvements, installation of renewable power applications, and methane recovery from waste management.

Milestone 5. Monitor and verify results. Monitoring and verifying progress on the implementation of measures to reduce or avoid greenhouse gas emissions is an ongoing process. Monitoring begins once measures are implemented and continues for the life of the measures, providing important feedback that can be use to improve the measures over time.

The five milestones provide a flexible framework that can accommodate varying levels of analysis, effort, and availability of data. This element makes the CCP both unique and innovative, by increasing its transferability amongst local governments. It is the breadth of this program that enables it to cross north/south, developed/developing, metropolis/town boundaries and that has made it successful worldwide.

Box 10   U.S. Mayors Climate Protection Agreement

Seattle Mayor Greg Nickels and the mayors of nine other cities introduced the U.S. Mayors Climate Protection Agreement to the U.S. Conference of Mayors on 13 June 2005, where it was adopted unanimously. As of 2008, over 800 mayors had signed the Agreement, representing all 50 states as well as the ten largest cities.
From City of Seattle, www.seattle.gov/mayor/climate

The U.S. Mayors Climate Protection Agreement

A. We urge the federal government and state governments to enact policies and programs to meet or beat the Kyoto Protocol target of reducing global warming pollution levels to 7% below 1990 levels by 2012, including efforts to reduce the United States' dependence on fossil fuels and accelerate the development of clean, economical energy resources and fuel-efficient technologies such as conservation, methane recovery for energy generation, wind and solar energy, fuel cells, efficient motor vehicles, and biofuels;

B. We urge the U.S. Congress to pass the bipartisan Climate Stewardship Act sponsored by Senators McCain and Lieberman and Representatives Gilchrist and Olver, which would create a flexible, market-based system of tradable allowances among emitting industries; and

C. We will strive to meet or exceed Kyoto Protocol targets for reducing global warming pollution by taking actions in our own operations and communities such as:

1. Inventory global warming emissions in City operations and in the community, set reduction targets and create an action plan.

2. Adopt and enforce land-use policies that reduce sprawl, preserve open space, and create compact, walkable urban communities;

3. Promote transportation options such as bicycle trails, commute trip reduction programs, incentives for car pooling and public transit;

4. Increase the use of clean, alternative energy by, for example, investing in "green tags", advocating for the development of renewable energy resources, and recovering landfill methane for energy production;

5. Make energy efficiency a priority through building code improvements, retrofitting city facilities with energy efficient lighting and urging employees to conserve energy and save money;

6. Purchase only Energy Star equipment and appliances for City use;

7. Practice and promote sustainable building practices using the U.S. Green Building Council's LEED program or a similar system;

8. Increase the average fuel efficiency of municipal fleet vehicles; reduce the number of vehicles; launch an employee education program including anti-idling messages; convert diesel vehicles to bio-diesel;

9. Evaluate opportunities to increase pump efficiency in water and wastewater systems; recover waste water treatment methane for energy production;

10. Increase recycling rates in City operations and in the community;

11. Maintain healthy urban forests; promote tree planting to increase shading and to absorb CO_2; and

12. Help educate the public, schools, other jurisdictions, professional associations, business and industry about reducing global warming pollution.

Adaptation and Next Steps

A series of unusually frequent and powerful storms and hurricanes in the late 1980s and early 1990s spurred analysts in the insurance industry to see a link between global warming and industry losses—earlier than even most governments. In November 1990, just a few months after the release of the first IPCC report, re-insurer giant Swiss Re noted that "a significant body of scientific evidence" suggested that recent losses "may be the result of climatic changes that will enormously expand the liability of the property-casualty industry."[54]

Despite this early recognition of the serious and immediate economic impacts of global warming, governments in general have tended to focus on mitigation.[55] However, adaptation has received increased a new surge of attention in the wake of the April 2007 IPCC Working Group II report, the most detailed report yet on the impacts of climate change and the need to identify vulnerabilities and adapt to unavoidable effects. The report described a wide range of global and regional impacts on both the environment and human society, including impacts related to health, water supplies, coastal areas, forests, agriculture, biodiversity and recreation (see *Box 11* for a summary of the report's findings for North America).

Despite a turnaround in mainstream U.S. political opinion on global warming between 2005 and 2007[56], and a recent surge of investment in energy-efficient technologies and renewable energy sources, U.S. governments still lag behind the rest of the industrialized world in both mitigation and adaptation planning. According to an April 2007 *Boston Globe* article, "only a handful of [U.S.] cities or states have begun projects or adopted regulations to accommodate higher temperatures, changing precipitation patterns, sea level rise, and longer growing seasons."[57]

Local efforts to adapt to climate change are particularly difficult as they must consider a complex set of environmental, economic and social relationships and impacts. A number of recent government reports—including those from Australia, Canada, and the European Union—identify risk management, adaptive management and system analysis as key approaches for integrating climate change adaptation into local government decision-making (see *Box 11* and *Box 12* for selected excerpts, and *Appendix: Resources* for selected references). As the fields of urban planning and urban management gradually integrate environmental science concepts like vulnerability, resilience, and complex adaptive systems,[58] new and better tools will emerge for systematically and comprehensively adapting to climate change.

Farmers and water resource managers have a long history of adapting to climate shocks and stresses. However, the current climate change phenomenon is projected to exacerbate these shocks and stresses, and result in long-term changes in precipitation and evaporation. Increasing our capacity to cope is imperative. Public policies can help build this capacity. However, a key challenge is developing policies that are robust enough to be useful in a rapidly changing and uncertain future.

- International Institute for Sustainable Development, et al. (2006) "Designing policies in a world of uncertainty, change, and surprise."

Projections of Global Surface Temperatures: Greenhouse Gas Emissions Scenarios

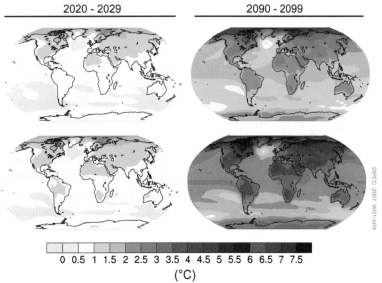

2020 - 2029   2090 - 2099

Scenario B1. Global solutions
Income and lifestyle trends converge globally
Rapid shift toward service/information economy
Global sustainability solutions
Clean, resource-efficient technologies
Population rising to 9 billion then declining

Scenario A1B. Global development
Income and lifestyle trends converge globally
Very rapid economic growth
More efficient technologies
Balance of all energy sources
Population rising to 9 billion then declining

©IPCC 2007 WG1-AR4

0 0.5 1 1.5 2 2.5 3 3.5 4 4.5 5 5.5 6 6.5 7 7.5
(°C)

Adapted from: Intergovernmental Panel on Climate Change, "Contribution of Working Group I to the Fourth Assessment Report: Summary for Policy Makers," February 2007, Geneva, Switzerland.

Box 11 Adapting to Global Warming: Impacts and Policy

North America: Impacts

Excerpted from a National Environmental Trust (NET) summary of the April 2007 Fourth Assessment Report by the Intergovernmental Panel on Climate Change-Working Group II (IPCC-WG2), which focused on the impacts of global warming. The full NET summary is available at www.net.org/warming, and the full IPCC report is available at www.ipcc.ch.

- Tens of million of Americans are likely to be exposed to greater risks for injury, disease and mortality due to higher pollution levels, more frequent and more intense heat waves, more intense storms, elevated pollen levels and better conditions for the spread of water- and insect-borne diseases, in the absence of effective counter-measures.

- Western and Southwestern states already facing increased water scarcity are expected to experience inadequate water supplies and reliability losses as snowpack diminishes and evaporation increases in both regions, with added stress in the Southwest caused by precipitation decreases.

- North American forests face escalating destruction from increasing outbreaks of wildfire, insect infestation and disease. Wood and timber producers could suffer losses of between $1 billion and $2 billion a year during the 21st century due to those disturbances.

- Coastal states face rising sea-levels accompanied by greater vulnerability to intense storms and storm surges, coastal erosion and gradual inundation, effects which will also contribute to wetland losses. Storm impacts are likely to be more severe, especially along the Gulf and Atlantic coasts, where any increase in destructiveness of coastal storms combined threatens significant increases in life and property losses.

- Between 15% and 40% of North American plant and animal species are likely to be condemned to extinction by 2050.

Europe: Vulnerability and Adaptation

Excerpted from "Vulnerability and adaptation to climate change in Europe," European Environment Agency, Copenhagen, 2006, page 8.

Development and implementation of adaptation measures is a relatively new issue. Existing adaptive measures are very much concentrated in flood defence, which has enjoyed a long tradition of dealing with weather extremes. Concrete adaptation policies, measures and practices outside this area are still scarce. Therefore, there is considerable scope for advancing adaptation planning and implementation in areas such as public health, water resources and management of ecosystems. There are a number of challenges which should be addressed to make progress on climate change adaptation. These include:

- improving climate models and scenarios at detailed regional level, especially for extreme weather events, to reduce the high level of uncertainty;

- advancing understanding on 'good practice' in adaptation measures through exchange and information sharing on feasibility, costs and benefits;

- involving the public and private sector, and the general public at both local and national levels;

- enhancing coordination and collaboration both within and between countries to ensure the coherence of adaptation measures with other policy objectives, and the allocation of appropriate resources.

Australia: Risk, Vulnerability and Adaptation

Excerpted from "Climate Change Risk and Vulnerability: Promoting an efficient adaptation response in Australia," Australian Greenhouse Office, Department of the Environment and Heritage, March 2005, page viii.

...Some sectors, like insurance and re–insurance, are already including climate risk in their decision making. Governments will need to consider the issues around the distribution of losses in the community arising from the possibility of either a withdrawal of insurance from covering some risks, a huge increase in costs, or the failure of one or more major companies...

...An adaptation strategy, to be effective, must result in climate risk being considered as a normal part of decision-making, allowing governments, businesses and individuals to reflect their risk preferences just as they would for other risk assessments. In this sense, adaptation strategies will fail if they continue in the long run to be seen in a 'silo' separate from other dimensions of strategic planning and risk management. To reach this point, however, is going to require a period of awareness raising, development of the science, and development of techniques for applying it in practical situations. This is a common path in developing public policy in 'new' fields. The first step is to identify priorities.

Box 12 Adapting to Global Warming: Local Functions

New Zealand: Local Government Preparedness

Excerpted from "Preparing for climate change: A guide for local government in New Zealand" New Zealand Climate Change Office, Ministry for the Environment, June 2004, page 24.

When assessing the possible effects of climate change on a particular council function or service it may be helpful to consider the extent to which council functions and services... depend on climate parameters. [This table is] designed to help council staff understand and qualitatively determine the role of climate, and hence climate change, for a wide range of council functions and services.

Table: Local government functions and possible climate change effects

Function	Affected assets or activities	Key climate influence	Possible effects	Sensitivity to Effects
Water supply and irrigation	Infrastructure	Reduced rainfall, extreme rainfall events; increased temperature	Reduced security of supply (depending on water source); contamination of water supply.	Rivers, groundwater, water quality, water availability, coastal areas
Wastewater	Infrastructure	Increased rainfall	More intense rainfall (extreme events) will cause more inflow and infiltration into wastewater network; wet weather overflow events will increase in frequency and volume; longer dry spells will increase likelihood of blockages and related dry weather overflows.	Drainage
Stormwater	Reticulation, stopbanks	Increased rainfall; rise in sea level	Increased frequency and/or volume of system flooding; increased peak flows in streams and related erosion; groundwater level changes; saltwater intrusion in coastal zones; changing flood plains and greater likelihood of damage to properties and infrastructure.	Rivers, drainage, coastal areas
Roading	Road network and associated infrastructure	Extreme rainfall events, extreme winds	Disruption due to flooding, landslides, fallen trees and lines; direct effects of wind exposure on heavy vehicles.	Drainage, natural hazards
Planning/policy development	Management of private sector development; urban expansion; infrastructure and communications planning	All	Inappropriate location of urban expansion areas; inadequate or inappropriate infrastructure, costly retrofitting of systems.	Rivers, groundwater, drainage, coastal areas, natural hazards
Landcare	Rural land management	Changes in rainfall, wind and temperature	Enhanced erosion; changes in type/distribution of pest species; increased fire risk; reduction in water availability for irrigation; changes in appropriate land use; changes in evapo-transpiration.	Water availability, erosion, biodiversity, biosecurity, natural hazards
Watercare	Management of watercourses/ lakes/ wetlands	Rainfall and temperature changes	More variation in water volumes possible; reduced water quality; sedimentation and weed growth; changes in type/distribution of pest species.	Rivers, lakes, wetlands, water quality, drainage, erosion, biosecurity
Coastal management	Infrastructure; management of coastal development	Temperature changes leading to sea level changes; extreme storm events	Coastal erosion and flooding; disruption in roading, communications; loss of private property and community assets; effects on water quality.	Coastal areas, natural hazards
Civil defence and emergency management	Emergency planning and response; recovery operations	Extreme events	Greater risks to public safety and to resources needed to manage flood, rural fire, landslip and storm events.	Natural hazards
Biosecurity	Pest management	Temperature/ rainfall changes	Changes in range of pest species.	Biosecurity, biodiversity
Open space and community facilities management	Planning and management of parks, playing fields and urban open spaces	Temperature/ rainfall changes; extreme wind and rainfall events	Changes/reduction in water availability; changes in biodiversity; changes in type/distribution of pest species; groundwater changes; saltwater intrusion in coastal zones; need for more shelter in urban spaces.	Groundwater, drainage, water availability, biodiversity, coastal areas
Transport	Management of public transport; provision of footpaths, cycleways etc	Changes in temperature, wind and rainfall	Changed maintenance needs for public transport (road, rail) infrastructure; disruption due to extreme events.	Drainage, natural hazards
Waste management	Transfer stations and landfills	Changes in rainfall and temperature	Increased surface flooding risk; biosecurity changes; changes in ground water level and leaching.	Biosecurity, natural hazards

5. Transitioning to the Post Carbon World

This final chapter develops the preceding ideas and lessons into a set of recommendations and a vision for transitioning to a world no longer dependent on hydrocarbon fuels nor emitting climate-changing levels of carbon: the post-carbon world.

Here we will:

— consider the deep challenges and unusual opportunities that cities now face,

— recommend four initial steps and five principles to guide cities in their responses to energy and climate uncertainty, and

— highlight the underlying message of this Guidebook, and introduce the strategy of "relocalization."

5.1 **Unprecedented challenges** We are entering a new age—a new *urban* age. The majority of the world's people now live in cities or suburbs. Never before have so many people been so dependent on faraway places for basic needs like food and fuel. At the same time, the very thing that has made this unprecedented global urbanization possible—our voracious consumption of oil and natural gas—has also given rise to peak oil and global warming, two enormous problems which threaten to wreak havoc with our globalized urban world if we don't address them quickly and forcefully.

For most of Western history we've held the notion that "Nature" is so vast that it can supply our fuel and absorb our waste without limit. In this new urban age of energy and climate uncertainty, however, there are new-found limits to what the planet can both provide and withstand, and serious consequences if we push those limits too far. We must discard our old notions of a limitless natural world, and adopt a worldview that places the highest possible value on the stewarding of our energy resources and our ecosystems.

Transition

The challenge to you, as a municipal leader or staff member, is formidable: if your city's transition into the new urban age is to be a smooth one, you and your fellow officials, planners and citizens must do no less than rethink, redesign and retrofit city and your local economy according to these new limits.

The transition to this new urban age will not be easy. Peak oil and climate change are very complicated issues that are already affecting modern civilization in ways not fully understood. They are not linear problems with quick fixes, but system problems that require continuing management and multiple approaches to navigate.

Your city must rethink, redesign and retrofit itself according to the limits of what the planet can provide and withstand.

The transition is not a choice, however. The new urban age of energy and climate uncertainty has already begun, and your city has a window of opportunity to prepare for its challenges now.

5.2 **Unusual opportunities** Local governments in the U.S. and Canada are well-suited to address these challenges, thanks to the influence they have on local land use, transportation and economic activities.

In fact, your city has a huge fiscal incentive for addressing peak oil and climate change: just about everything you do to reduce energy consumption and carbon emissions in your city will save money in the long run. The challenges of peak oil and climate change are *opportunities* for your city to build local wealth and improve its quality of life.

Consider some of the actions cities are regularly urged to take in the name of energy efficiency and sustainability:

- Reduce car use by **building vibrant, mixed-use, walkable urban neighborhoods.**

- Boost local jobs and reduce the distances consumer goods travel by **developing the local manufacturing base.**

- Reduce energy waste by **improving building quality** through better insulation, ventilation and solar access.

Just about everything you do to reduce energy consumption and carbon emissions in your city will save money in the long run.

- Reduce the distances food must travel by **protecting regional farmland and developing local agriculture.**

- Generate energy from clean and secure sources by **developing local wind power, solar power, distributed generation and regional biofuel production.**

- Develop free "ecosystem services" like stormwater mitigation and wildlife habitat by **rebuilding wetlands, building bioswales and planting street trees.**

Rather than struggling with a future of energy poverty, our cities can build thriving futures of energy prudence. The technology and the design practices already exist to transform cities from net energy *losers*—powered by fossil fuels and damaging the very ecosystems that support them—to net energy *gainers* that produce their own energy and actually regenerate healthy local ecosystems.

How is this possible? Didn't we try conservation and alternative energy in the 1970s, only to arrive at this energy and climate predicament today? Yes, but now there are three key differences:

- **We have the technologies we need.** In the 1970s, solar, wind and biofuels were "boutique" energy sources, with minimal government support and marginal returns on investment. Today these energy technologies are greatly improved and increasingly used worldwide to reliably power vehicles, factories and entire city districts. Other

High-performance buildings should be the norm... Municipal governments have a huge role to play in bringing about that progress.

- Salt Lake City Mayor Rocky Anderson, quoted in Neal Peirce, "Sustainable Cities," The American Prospect, 7 Jan 2007

modern technologies, like combined heat and power (CHP), hybrid electric engines and green building practices are producing significant energy efficiencies at competitive prices.

- **We know much more about managing resource supply and demand.** Over the last few decades, a number of innovative management, engineering and design approaches have emerged for conserving resources while saving money and improving services. Soft path analysis, ecological design principles, "Factor Four" guidelines, "The Natural Step" and other approaches make up a growing knowledge base for us to more intelligently use the resources on which we depend.[59]

- **We know what to build and how to build it.** Today's "green" cities in Western Europe were just starting to experiment with alternative energy, car-free urban design and other sustainability practices in the 1960s and 70s. Today we can learn from nearly half a century of modern European "best practices," as well as decades of experience in applying these ideas in North America.

We also have another opportunity: Whether this growth is desired or not, in twenty-five years the U.S. and Canada will likely have around 70 million more people than today.[60] We and all of these additional people will need housing and transportation. We can take advantage of the huge economic investments that will meet these needs to redesign our cities as sustainable net energy producers.

5.3 **What your city can do** What should your city do to transition smoothly into the new urban age of energy and climate uncertainty? Of all the tasks at hand, which should you do first, and which are the most important in the long run?

In developing this guidebook we consulted with dozens of elected officials, managers, planners, architects, scientists and scholars with these questions in mind. Drawing from these valuable conversations, as well as the experiences of American and Canadian municipalities that have already started addressing peak oil and climate change, we advise the following four steps and five principles, all discussed in detail below:

Take these *four initial steps* immediately:

1. **Sign the Mayors Climate Protection Agreement and/or endorse the World Mayors and Municipal Leaders Declaration on Climate Change.**
2. **Join the Cities for Climate Protection Campaign.**
3. **Sign the Oil Depletion Protocol.**
4. **Establish a Peak Oil Task Force.**

Integrate these *five principles* into your municipality's decision-making and long-range planning processes.

1. **Deal with transportation and land use (or you may as well stop now).**
2. **Tackle private energy consumption.**
3. **Attack the problems piece-by-piece and from many angles.**
4. **Plan for fundamental changes...and make fundamental changes happen.**
5. **Build a sense of community.**

What can we do? We can invest in a flexible transportation with many non-automobile options. We can re-zone our communities so that jobs are close to housing. We can adopt new standards requiring sidewalks everywhere, and better connectivity. We can talk to our citizens about how we need to be prudent and wise and prepare for the inevitable switch to a less petroleum-intensive lifestyle. We can talk about the opportunities for greater social engagement, healthier lives and cleaner air that such a change can bring, if we plan and invest wisely in our communities' future.

The thing we can't do is stick our heads in the sand, or wait for Congress to finally agree to do something.

- Councilmember Rex Burkholder, Metro (regional government), Portland, Oregon

Transition

Step 1. Sign the Mayors Climate Protection Agreement (U.S.) and/or endorse the World Mayors and Municipal Leaders Declaration on Climate Change.
Set greenhouse gas reduction targets.

Under the U.S. Mayors Climate Protection Agreement (see *Box 10*, page 54), launched when the Kyoto Protocol went into effect in February 2005, participating U.S. cities commit to meeting Kyoto targets for greenhouse gas reductions in the absence of federal leadership. The World Mayors and Municipal Leaders Declaration on Climate Change, adopted in a parallel municipal leaders summit at the December 2005 United Nations Climate Change Conference, calls for cities to have a stronger voice in international climate protection.

Signing the Agreement (U.S. cities) and/or the Declaration (U.S. and Canadian cities) sends an important statement to your staff and community—as well as state/provincial and federal governments—that your city is committed to serious action on climate change. It will also connect you to a growing national network of municipal leaders and a campaign to urge federal action on carbon mitigation efforts.

Visit www.coolmayors.com to sign the Agreement and www.iclei.org/montrealsummit for more information about the Declaration.

Step 2. Join the Cities for Climate Protection Campaign.
Reduce greenhouse gas emissions.

Since 1993, over 800 local governments around the world have joined the Cities for Climate Protection Campaign organized by ICLEI-Local Governments for Sustainability.[61] This program is a five-step framework for municipalities to integrate greenhouse gas reductions into local decision-making (see *Box 9*, page 53).

Joining the Cities for Climate Protection Campaign will get you started with immediate actions to reduce energy use and greenhouse gas emissions. It will also connect you to the resources and expertise of the leading global network of local governments working on climate change.

Visit www.iclei.org to join the Campaign.

Step 3. Sign the Oil Depletion Protocol.
Set oil consumption reduction targets.

The Oil Depletion Protocol is a relatively new international agreement to avoid price and supply volatility problems associated with global oil production decline by gradually and collaboratively lowering the global rate of oil production and oil consumption.

Much as the Kyoto Protocol is inspiring many cities to work locally towards global carbon mitigation targets, the Oil Depletion Protocol is inspiring cities to set local targets for reducing oil consumption. Signing the Oil Depletion Protocol signals your city's commitment to reducing its energy vulnerability, and connects you to a growing international network of governments and institutions that are organizing to dampen the effects of peak oil.

Visit www.oildepletionprotocol.org to sign the Protocol and see *Appendix: Making a government statement on peak oil* (page 70) to get started.

Step 4. Establish a Peak Oil Task Force.
Identify and reduce peak oil vulnerabilities.

The decision-makers and staff of your city need to understand the significance of peak oil and the deep challenges it will create. It's especially important that they recognize any vulnerabilities specific to your city's economic and geographical context.

Establishing a Peak Oil Task Force will enable your city to quickly identify these challenges and vulnerabilities. You'll need this information to integrate energy uncertainty considerations into municipal activities. It's also a valuable way to introduce businesses, citizens and other community stakeholders to the challenges of energy uncertainty, and engage them in developing a broad-based response.

See *Appendix: Establishing a peak oil task force* (page 73) to get started.

> We have built a pattern over the last 50 years that is 99.9% automobile-dependent, as government policy; in fact, we've subsidized it. The difficulty is that the pattern has now been so ingrained that the changes we need to make are going to have be done on a gradual basis over, perhaps, the next 50 years.
>
> In the meantime it's fairly clear, whether we like to admit it or not, that Canada and the United States simply will not be able to compete with the levels of efficiency of Asian cities and Scandinavian cities.
>
> - Anton Nelessen, architect, A. Nelessen Associates, Princeton, New Jersey

Post Carbon Cities: Five Principles

In taking those first four steps, your city will begin systematically reducing its energy use and greenhouse gas emissions, starting a smooth transition to the new urban age of energy and climate uncertainty.

The following five principles are essential to continuing this smooth transition. Integrate these principles in your municipality's ongoing decision-making and long-range planning processes:

1. Deal with transportation and land use (or you may as well stop now). [62]

We've built most of our cities and suburbs in such a way that it is nearly impossible to meet even basic needs without using enormous amounts of petroleum-based fuels. Governments of all sizes need to use their land use and transportation planning powers to make walking, bicycling and public transit more convenient and more sensible choices than driving. Until then, most of us will have little choice but to remain dependent on an increasingly scarce, expensive and climate-changing energy source just to get around.

The built-in oil dependency of our cities and suburbs is the biggest obstacle to significantly reducing our energy use. Our dependence will increasingly threaten local economic health as the price of oil rises and becomes more volatile. Those cities and suburbs that have redesigned themselves for the post-peak oil world will succeed, while other localities will find it more and more expensive to move people and goods around.

Incorporate peak oil and climate change in your long-range land use and transportation planning assumptions now. Don't just tinker with zoning codes and transportation funding—take the time and commit the resources to make serious changes:

- *Fundamentally rethink your municipality's land use and transportation practices,* from building and zoning codes to long-range planning. Are your regulations and procedures encouraging developers to build the best possible buildings and neighborhoods for a world without cheap oil? Are you discouraging the kinds of developments that will function poorly when gasoline is three times as expensive as today?

- *Make land use and transportation infrastructure decisions with 100 year time-frames.* What are the energy and mobility assumptions going into your current big infrastructure investments? Are you planting the seeds for energy-prudent land use patterns?

- *Organize with neighboring jurisdictions* to address these challenges at a regional level. Are you integrating cities and suburbs in a regional transportation plan? Are you protecting farmland and industrial areas throughout the region?

2. Tackle private energy consumption.

The vast majority of the urban energy footprint comes from private consumption, and a huge part of that comes from heating, cooling, and lighting buildings, and heating water. Reducing government consumption is an important step, but it will do very little to reduce overall community energy vulnerability without similar reductions in the private sector.

Local governments do not have direct control over consumer energy use, but they do have a powerful set of tools to influence the private sector, including zoning codes, buildings codes, business licenses, and public bonding power. And as a representative of a public body-whether as an elected official or a municipal staffer-your personal initiative and leadership automatically carry influence in your community.

We're building buildings with 50 year lifespans. We can make decisions for the long term and lead by example, and change the private sector.

- Mayor Derek Corrigan, City of Burnaby, British Columbia

Box 13   "Wedge" Strategies

Climate "Stabilization Wedges" Strategy (Pacala & Socolow)

Under the "stabilization wedges" strategy developed by Princeton professors Stephen Pacala and Robert Socolow, we can stabilize global carbon emissions (i.e., avoid future increases) by pursuing a number of limited emissions-mitigating actions, instead of putting enormous effort into a few "big fixes." Each "wedge" represents future carbon emissions avoided by pursuing one specific activity or technology, such as sequestering carbon underground, or improving automobile fuel efficiency. The wedges together make up a triangle representing the future increase of global carbon emissions that would occur over the coming decades if we do nothing. Pacala and Socolow identified more wedges than would be needed to stabilize carbon emissions over the next 50 years. Each wedge uses existing and proven technologies.

See http://www.princeton.edu/~cmi.

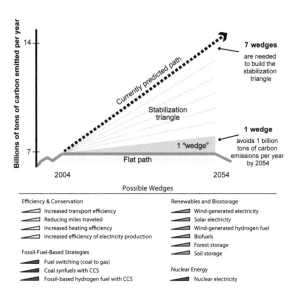

GRAPHIC: Carbon Mitigation Initiative, Princeton University.

Energy and Emissions Wedge Strategy (Davidson)

In his energy and emissions wedge strategy, Vancouver, B.C. architect Bryn Davidson addresses the coming gap between increasing energy demand and decreasing conventional oil and natural gas supply. Rising energy prices will result in limited reductions in energy demand and limited increases of non-conventional fossil fuel production. Davidson proposes that the remainder of the gap can be filled through proactive policies and design practices that reduce energy demand, and by developing clean energy sources to create new supply. This strategy would both reduce carbon emissions below current levels and avoid serious economic instability resulting from energy demand excessively outpacing supply.

See http://www.dynamiccities.org.

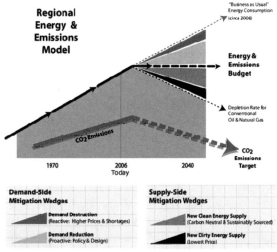

GRAPHIC: B. Davidson.

- *Use the tools you already have* to encourage serious energy conservation and efficiency in the private sector. Create strong incentives and support for innovations like zero-energy buildings[63], combined heat and power (CHP) systems, and industrial symbiosis[64]. Lead by example in your public projects and public-private partnerships.

- *Engage the business community aggressively.* Resource efficiency saves money, and new "green" industrial and business practices are a growing opportunity for economic development. Challenge your local business leaders to reinvent the local economy for the post-carbon world.

3. Attack the problems piece-by-piece and from many angles.

Princeton professors Stephen Pacala and Robert Socolow proposed a multiple-approach strategy for mitigating climate change in 2004[65], and Vancouver architect Bryn Davidson has recently proposed a similar strategy for responding to peak oil (see *Box 13*). While they differ in their particulars, the authors of both strategies demonstrate that any realistic reduction of carbon emissions or oil consumption requires multiple solutions—described as "wedges"—because no single solution can alone achieve the vast reductions needed.

By combining many solutions, you can reduce your city's dependence on fossil fuels using existing practices and technologies, to reduce demand and increase supply:

- *Meet your goals with multiple, proven solutions.* Don't look for a few "big fixes" on energy and greenhouse gases. Instead, pursue many different kinds of solutions at different scales, from promoting individual energy efficiency to rethinking the fundamentals of your regional economy.

- *Enlist the entire community.* Set clear community goals and then spur action from all sides—supply and demand, public and private, household and business—to meet them.

4. Plan for fundamental changes...and make fundamental changes happen.

Peak oil and global warming will fundamentally alter the way our modern globalized world works. Some change in the climate is now inevitable, and a huge amount of change in our energy supply is both inevitable and imminent.

The challenges of energy and climate uncertainty require us to approach how we manage our cities very differently than we have in the past. The current culture of city management, planning and development operates on a set of assumptions about energy and climate that must change quickly.

- *Educate and involve your fellow elected officials and staff* about the challenges of energy and climate uncertainty, and the need to change their operating assumptions accordingly. These are the people who will be guiding your community through the coming crises: raise their awareness of the problems and they will be better prepared to come up with the solutions.

- *Educate and involve your stakeholders,* which include business leaders, real estate developers, planners, architects, landowners, financers, engineers, community leaders, and citizens. Make sure they understand the seriousness of the challenges at hand, and challenge them to come up with serious solutions.

- *Lead your city's transition* by integrating peak oil and climate change considerations in your own decision-making. See to it that every project you are involved with smoothes the transition and reduces energy and climate vulnerability.

Transition

5. Build a sense of community.

Of all five principles, the most important has nothing to do with big renewable energy projects or complex zoning regulations. The fifth principle is to **build and nurture a greater sense of community in your city.**

The healthiest and most successful cities have a strong sense of community: strong relationships tie together individuals, neighborhoods, places of worship, schools, businesses, and City Hall. These relationships are the lifeblood of the community—without them, we start to lose civic engagement, community memory, local economic resilience, the willingness to help those not related to us, and many other qualities that make a city work well.

Neighborhoods with a strong sense of community are usually the ones that fare best in the long run: citizens, businesses and local institutions help each other weather short-term challenges, and they organize to meet long-term challenges. The knowledge, skills, experiences, and social capital of a strong community contribute more to a city's resilience over time than any multi-million dollar infrastructure project.

More than anything else, the resilience that comes from a strong sense of community will help your city meet the challenges of energy and climate uncertainty.

Build a sense of community throughout your city's neighborhoods:

- strengthen the city's neighborhood associations;
- protect neighborhood-scale schools, and set up community-school partnership programs
- allow a mix of uses in both buildings and neighborhoods;
- protect affordable housing, and allow accessory dwellings ("granny flats");
- develop a community policing program;
- encourage street fairs and farmers markets;
- build public squares to encourage public interaction;

In short, do anything you can to get people talking with each other, forming relationships, and investing themselves in the larger community. It's one of the least expensive things a local government can do. Done well, it's one of the most fruitful.

5.4   **The Bottom Line** Peak oil and climate change require urgent action. At current rates of fossil fuel consumption we will most likely pass peak oil by 2010, and we seriously risk widespread, catastrophic climate change if we do not begin dramatically reducing global carbon emissions immediately[66]. We need to act quickly and decisively.

To break dependence on oil, stop contributing to global warming, and build resilient cities that can thrive in the new urban age of energy and climate uncertainty, the bottom line for local governments is this: *"Reduce consumption, and produce locally."*

We in the United States and Canada consume far more goods and energy per person than the rest of the world's people, and much of that consumption is waste that can be avoided. Everything we consume has a financial and an ecological cost in its production, transport, use and disposal—costs that can be reduced to the benefit of the local economy and the global ecosystem.

> **To break dependence on oil, stop contributing to global warming, and build resilient cities that can thrive in the new urban age of energy and climate uncertainty, the bottom line for local governments is this: "Reduce consumption, and produce locally."**

Whether it's electricity, gasoline, shoes, meat, water, or ice cream, work to reduce your community's overall consumption and its dependence on faraway places for basic goods. The more your community can get its food, energy and basic manufactured goods from local sources, the less vulnerable it will be to rising and unstable oil prices, and the less it will contribute to climate change.

At Post Carbon Institute, we call this community resilience-building strategy *"relocalization."* Since 2003 we have been building an international network of citizen groups relocalizing their own communities (see www.relocalize.net). Many of these groups have been at the forefront of municipal efforts to identify and reduce local vulnerabilities arising from energy and climate uncertainty.

In 2007 we launched the Post Carbon Cities program to help local governments address the challenges of peak oil and climate change, and develop their own relocalization strategies. The Post Carbon Cities network is a resource for anyone who works with or for local governments. Our website at www.postcarboncities.net provides news and featured content, resources for policy and planning, and a forum for discussing challenges, best practices and lessons learned with other professionals and elected officials.

We welcome your participation; we can learn much more, much faster, by sharing our successes and our failures, building an ever-richer knowledge base. Please visit us online and join the growing movement of municipal leaders who are preparing their communities for the challenges of energy and climate uncertainty.

Appendix

CONTENTS

Making a government statement on peak oil 70

Establishing a peak oil task force 73

Systems Thinking: A Tool for Municipalities 79

Resources 85

Endnotes 91

Photo credits 95

Appendix

I would say that most city planners are aware of our energy predicament. The biggest hurdle facing the city planners is that they're so swamped with the day-to-day workload... it's really hard for them to put aside enough time to devote to thinking about how they're going to handle new trends in city design...

I'm in a really lucky position right now. Our city is progressive-thinking, and our City Council is very supportive; they've given me some support and direction to work on [energy independence]... We have a very limited budget so they can't commit huge amounts of time and money, but they're not afraid to take a position on it.

– Alan Falleri, Director of Community Development, City of Willits, California

Making a government statement on peak oil

This section will help you (a municipal elected official or staff member) develop a way for your local government to make an official statement on peak oil that is appropriate to your local context.

A good way for a community to start engaging the challenges of peak oil is for the local government to officially recognize the problem in some way. This may be as simple as an internal staff report, as public as a special Town Hall meeting, or as high-profile as a City Council establishing a study commission.

A municipal statement gives a sense of direction, legitimacy and momentum to what could otherwise be an unfocused and contentious policymaking process. Such a statement can serve two goals:

- *Raising awareness*
  Most citizens and businesses are aware that there is some connection between world events and the prices they pay for energy, but few pay close attention to the details of global oil supply and demand. Official municipal recognition of peak oil and energy uncertainty alerts the community to the fact that the issues even exist. The more households and businesses know about their community's oil and natural gas vulnerabilities, the more they will understand local government efforts to address them, and the better they will be able to mitigate community vulnerabilities privately.

  Local officials and staff in particular need to be made aware of energy uncertainty, and encouraged to think creatively about what it may mean for the municipal functions they are responsible for. You might consider holding a special staff presentation or workshop on the topic. The depth and success of the city's response to energy uncertainty will largely depend on the support the effort has from managers and staff.

- *Getting the ball rolling*
  Having some official acknowledgement of peak oil gives it legitimacy as an issue requiring municipal attention. It also sends municipal officials, staff and community members an important signal of support, enabling them to confidently begin working on this potentially controversial issue. This signal is especially important for staff in smaller jurisdictions, as limited resources often mean that non-immediate needs like long-term planning, forecasting and risk management won't get much attention without a clear indication of support from officials.

Here are two examples of what some municipalities have done to make a statement on peak oil:

- *Resolution*
  A resolution passed by the elected body sends a strong message to both staff and the community about the seriousness of the peak oil problem. A resolution can also formally set a direction for municipal response.

  - On April 28, 2006, the City of San Francisco passed a resolution recognizing the "critical" importance of affordable petroleum to the economy. It explicitly acknowledged the "unprecedented challenges of Peak Oil," and supported a city-wide assessment "with the aim of developing a comprehensive plan of action and response to Peak Oil." It also urged the Mayor to fund and direct the plan's development. (See *Box 14.*)

  - On July 20, 2006, the City of Bloomington (Indiana) passed a resolution recognizing the "severe impact" petroleum scarcity would have on the economy. Among its statements are that the City Council:

    - "acknowledges the unprecedented challenge of peak global petroleum production,"

    - "recognizes that the City of Bloomington must prepare for the inevitability of oil peak, and encourages the community to become better informed on energy-related matters."

    - "supports adoption of a global depletion protocol," and

    - "directs the City Clerk to distribute this Resolution to [Indiana's state and Federal elected officials], and urges them to take action on the impending peak in petroleum production and prepare for its consequences."

    See www.postcarboncities.net/node/180.

- *Report or White Paper*
  An internal report or policy paper can quickly establish a basis for addressing energy uncertainty, and open space for further and more in-depth study and assessment:

  - At the City of Burnaby (British Columbia), a January 2006 report on energy supply has helped raise awareness about the issue internally and has been used to provide back-

Box 14 San Francisco (Calif.) Peak Oil Resolution

This resolution, passed by the San Francisco Board of Supervisors on 11 April 2006, acknowledges the challenge of peak oil and the need for San Francisco to prepare a plan of response and preparation. Available online at http://www.sfgov.org/site/uploadedfiles/bdsupvrs/resolutions06/r0224-06.pdf.

Resolution acknowledging the challenge of Peak Oil and the need for San Francisco to prepare a plan of response and preparation.

WHEREAS, World oil production is nearing its point of maximum production ("Peak Oil") and will enter a prolonged period of irreversible decline leading to ever-increasing prices; and

WHEREAS, The United States has only 2 percent of the world's oil reserves, produces 8 percent of the world's oil and consumes 25 percent of the world's oil, of which nearly 60 percent is imported from foreign countries; and,

WHEREAS, The decline in global oil production threatens to increase resource competition, geopolitical instability, and lead to greater impoverishment; and,

WHEREAS, national oil companies own 72% of remaining oil reserves and 55% of remaining gas reserves, and resource nationalism is increasingly dominating decisions of oil and gas development and trade relationships; and,

WHEREAS, The availability of affordable petroleum is critical to the functioning of our transportation system, the production of our food and of petrochemical-based consumer goods, the paving of roads, the lubrication of all machinery, and myriad other parts of the economy; and,

WHEREAS, San Francisco is entirely dependent on external supplies of petroleum, including the crude oil processed in Bay Area refineries; and,

WHEREAS, Price signals of petroleum scarcity are likely to come too late to trigger effective mitigation efforts in the private sector, and governmental intervention at all levels of government will be required to avert social and economic chaos; and,

WHEREAS, The Department of Energy-sponsored study on mitigation of Peak Oil demonstrated that a twenty-year lead time is required for effective mitigation, while current measures supported by the federal government will replace only three weeks worth of gasoline consumption by 2012; and,

WHEREAS, Alternative sources of transport fuels from coal and natural gas both require high energy inputs and increase total carbon emissions, and biomass-based fuels compete with soil fertility, impacting agricultural sustainability; and,

WHEREAS, Substitution of petroleum with other fossil fuels threatens even greater damage to water, air, oil, and species diversity through the extraction and combustion; and,

WHEREAS, North American production of natural gas has already peaked, and 46% of California's electricity supply is generated from natural gas; and,

WHEREAS, San Francisco has demonstrated leadership in confronting challenges of environmental quality and energy security, promoting environmental and economic equity, and has a rich diversity of citizens committed to maintaining San Francisco's long-term viability; now, therefore, be it

RESOLVED, That the Board of Supervisors of the City and County of San Francisco acknowledges the unprecedented challenges of Peak Oil; and, be it

FURTHER RESOLVED, That the Board of Supervisors supports the adoption of a global Oil Depletion Protocol to provide transparency in oil markets, control price swings, address issues of equity in access to remaining oil resources, and provide a framework of predictability within which municipal governments can adjust to increasing oil scarcity; and be it

FURTHER RESOLVED, That the Board of Supervisors supports the undertaking of a city-wide assessment study in order to inventory city activities and their corollary resource requirements, evaluating the impact in each area of a decline in petroleum availability and of higher prices, with the aim of developing a comprehensive city plan of action and response to Peak Oil; and, be it

FURTHER RESOLVED, That the Board of Supervisors urges the Mayor to provide funding and direction to city departments for the development of a response plan.

ground on certain City Council decisions, such as the promotion of bicycling infrastructure and opposition to freeway widening.
Available at http://www.postcarboncities.net/node/164.

- The City of Hamilton (Ontario), commissioned a report to broadly consider how the municipality might approach future energy constraints. The April 2006 report proposed specific goals and opportunities for energy use and production, and has given city officials a useful framework for bringing together programs on energy, air quality and carbon mitigation initiatives.
Available at http://www.postcarboncities.net/node/267.

- At Metro, the regional government of the Portland (Oregon) metropolitan area, an April 2006 policy white paper on future "oil supply uncertainty" related this issue to specific Metro responsibilities, establishing a basis for further assessment and future responses. Metro Council's acceptance of the white paper got the issue favorable coverage on the front page of the daily business newspaper.
Available at http://www.metro-region.org/article.cfm?ArticleID = 18951

See www.postcarboncities.net/resources for a regularly-updated collection of local government resolutions, ordinances and reports related to energy uncertainty.

Establishing a peak oil task force

This section will help you (a municipal elected official or staff member) develop a volunteer-based task force to inquire into the vulnerabilities your community faces in peak oil, and to develop recommendations for response actions.

A peak oil task force investigates the ways in which your community is dependent on oil and natural gas.

Mapping this dependency can be surprisingly difficult task; it requires more than just a list of all the ways oil is used in the community (see *Systems Thinking: A Tool for Municipalities* on page 79 for an in-depth discussion of identifying vulnerabilities in complex systems). This process can be complicated if you don't have a clearly-defined structure, process and goal to guide your inquiry.

Below are some suggestions for organizing and running a peak oil task force, based on the experiences of the cities discussed in Section 4.1. The actual scope and structure of your inquiry, however, will depend on the size of your community, the available resources and your ultimate goals.

Organizing the task force

Recruit the right members and staff

When the City of Portland set up its Peak Oil Task Force in 2006, the City's Office of Sustainable Development used an interview and referral process to ensure they were selecting people who knew their fields and knew how to work effectively in a collaborative group process. The Portland task force also benefited greatly from having a few City staff on hand to assist the process and assemble technical data, allowing members to concentrate on interviewing experts, researching impacts and digesting information.

There can be problems with volunteer task forces, however, including lack of clear direction, disruptive volunteers, and lack of time. While the organization and execution of any special inquiry must be done with care, municipalities should be especially mindful when undertaking volunteer-staffed inquiries to avoid wasting people's time.

—**TIP: Involve key staff and influential community members in discussions right from the start.**
Don't just rely on interested volunteers: recruit the editor of a local newspaper, the owner of an important local company, and the leader of a local religious or minority community. In addition to your own municipality's staff, consider involving key staff from neighboring or overlapping jurisdictions. The right mix of leaders, advocates and staff will add expertise, open doors and increase the credibility of your task force.

Define the problem

If you plan to launch a peak oil task force you will need a clear problem statement. Otherwise, it's easy for the people working on it to end up thinking about the problem in divergent ways, or to get too caught up in details.

Municipalities need to address peak oil and energy uncertainty in ways appropriate to unique local needs, resources and context. For example, one community may see peak oil as a threat to affordable gasoline; another may see it as a broad threat to their regional economic competitiveness; and yet another may need to focus all its attention on urgent electricity or heating and cooling needs. Whatever the objective, a clear, documented statement of the problem or objective will keep participants focused.

Define the process and the goals

Once you've defined the problem, you need to get everyone together on the process. Announcing the start of an organized process is an opportunity to tell staff and community members how they can contribute and toward what end. Are you undertaking a comprehensive, community-wide energy assessment, or developing an oil price shock contingency plan? Will your community want a long-term initiative to develop sustainability across all sectors, or is there only support for an ad hoc committee to find potential cost savings in energy diversification?

Structuring the inquiry

As mentioned above, the way you define the problem will help guide how the task force approaches it. In the same fashion, the way the task force structures its inquiry will define what kinds of information it will find and what conclusions it will reach. Thus it's very important to structure the inquiry with its end product in mind. For example:

The first thing is to take stock. What kind of dependency do we have on the importation of materials and energy for the community, and what can we do locally—what can we do to relocalize?

- Councilmember Dave Rollo, City of Bloomington, Indiana

Appendix

- **Departmental inquiry.** Are you only interested in identifying potential fiscal vulnerabilities of official municipal responsibilities? Then you may want to organize an internal assessment divided by department, with a focus on potential cost scenarios and clear roles for managers and staff to drive the process.

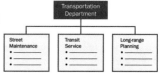

- **Sectoral inquiry.** Are you interested in general vulnerabilities of the entire community? Then you may want to establish a volunteer citizens commission and divide your assessment into broad areas like "Transportation," "Local Economy," and "Food." You'll need to carefully consider how to deal with challenges like overlapping data, and structure the inquiry in such a way that you don't get overwhelmed with information from the volunteer committees.

There are many different ways you can structure the inquiry. Risk analysts in the insurance industry use categorized checklists to identify vulnerabilities in well-understood conditions. On the other hand, a "blank slate" approach that uses brainstorming, expert interviews and multiple discussion rounds may be more appropriate for situations where there are more unknowns.

Identify crucial information needs early so you can structure your inquiry in the most useful way. If your community has one major employer, or is extremely dependent on one kind of trade or one mode of transportation, you will want to plan extra time for investigating the vulnerabilities that may affect such key points.

Be sure to enlist the help of the people who know your community and its economy intimately: agency managers and staff, business owners, community leaders, professors and researchers from a local college, etc. Whether as committee members or as interview subjects, nobody knows the specific challenges that volatile oil and gas prices may present to different sectors better than the people who work with them on a daily basis.

—**TIP: Have a clear structure for your assessment.**
Are you dividing up areas of inquiry into sectors like land use, food and economy, or by municipal responsibilities like emergency services, planning and public finance? How are you dealing with issues that fall into multiple categories? How are you differentiating between immediate needs and long-term needs?

—**TIP: Keep scoping, analysis, and solutions separate.**
It's easy to start talking about impacts, risks and potential responses all at the same time. Make sure you're not talking about possible responses until you've actually identified your community's most important vulnerabilities.

Running the inquiry

Start big

Before you begin asking detailed questions you should first collect basic supply and demand information from a "high altitude." You'll need this information to understand how the potential impacts of energy uncertainty will specifically affect your community. How are oil, motor fuels and natural gas delivered to your area? What agency or corporation operates the delivery infrastructure? If there is a shortage, who gets cut off first? What and who are the biggest users of oil and gas in your community?

Then move on to the most basic functions in your community: How does your food get there? Where is your main water supply? Where does your electricity come from and who controls the transmission infrastructure? What are the main industries in your community? As you collect information you may find you need to adjust the structure of your inquiry: for example, instead of one committee looking broadly at the local economy it may make more sense to split the effort between the traded sector (export-oriented) and non-traded sector (local market-oriented).

—**TIP: Identify key questions and information needs early.**
Is your local economy centered on a key industry? Talk to a representative business leader and learn what *their* vulnerabilities might be. Is your community expecting a lot of growth and new construction? Find out how current regulations are shaping the land use and transportation patterns that new development will produce.

Be comprehensive

The more wide-ranging your inquiry is, the better chance you'll have of capturing all the possible vulnerabilities that may affect your community. Identify the main influences on local economic, land use and transportation patterns. Don't think immediately in terms of oil and natural gas—oil and gas affect just about everything, so if you focus too narrowly at the outset, you may well miss an important vulnerability later on that at first didn't seem to have anything to do with oil or gas. Look especially to basic systems like water, sewer and emergency services.

Follow leads

As you develop a broad picture of your community's reliance on oil and natural gas, you can gradually determine where best to focus your assessment efforts. You may also come across intriguing information that points to unsuspected vulnerabilities. Take the time to look (if only briefly) into these tangents to see if they warrant further investigation: a key part of uncovering how a complex system works is following the leads that take us to something we didn't see before.

—**TIP: Avoid getting sidetracked.** Since oil and natural gas affect everything from the structure of the global economy to the way we go about our daily lives, it's easy to get sidetracked on details and "potluck conversation." Save discussions about the geopolitics of oil or the intricacies of plastics manufacturing for after the meeting, and keep your assessment focused on the impacts and vulnerabilities specific to your community.

Analyzing vulnerabilities

The goal of this step is to have the information from your inquiry digested and organized enough so that people can start making informed, grounded decisions about responses. In other words, you're not trying to uncover *every* vulnerability in your community, but rather you're trying to paint a clear enough picture of impacts and their potential ramifications so that leaders of agencies, departments, businesses, and neighborhoods have a basis for thinking through their own vulnerabilities and possible responses. Concentrate on the systems and the relationships.

To get the information to that useable point there are three kinds of analysis that are helpful: *digging in* to what you've collected so you can identify more specific vulnerabilities; *categorizing* vulnerabilities so that you can organize them in a way that is more in line with how you may actually respond to them; and *ranking* your vulnerabilities to indicate possible priorities for action. Again, depending on the structure and goals of your overall effort, there are different ways you might approach this step and different methods you may choose. The important thing is to process the information from your inquiry to make it as useful as possible and to ensure that it accurately and thoroughly describes your community's situation.

Digging in

It's easy to predict that higher oil prices will impact people's ability to drive, or that higher natural gas prices will impact people's ability to heat their homes—but how do we dig deeper to be sure we're developing a comprehensive picture of our vulnerabilities? There are many methods available for assessing the implications of risk and uncertainty, and we can use different methods to learn different things. Let's look at two methods that will give us different but useful results: (1) thinking through general impacts of different scenarios, and (2) thinking through the different levels of impact on one sector:

- **Scenarios.** The problem at hand is oil and gas price *volatility and increases*, so to capture an appropriately wide range of possible impacts it can be helpful to imagine different scenarios of oil price and supply. "What challenges might the community face if the price of oil gradually rose to $100 per barrel over the following year? How might those challenges be different if oil prices jumped erratically between $50 and $200 over the next ten years? What would happen if there was a natural gas shortage in February?" Then you can think about how the actors, functions and systems you identified in your inquiry might respond.

Scenario A	Scenario B	Scenario C
Impact A1	Impact B1	Impact C1
Impact A2	Impact B2	Impact C2
Impact A3	Impact B3	Impact C3
Impact A4	Impact B4	Impact C4
Impact A5	Impact B5	Impact C5
Impact A6	Impact B6	Impact C6
Impact A7	Impact B7	Impact C7

> **You can run a bowling ball across the entire city [of Canby], so there are no advantages of putting a big water tank up on a hill. To have pressure in that town you have to run pumps.**
>
> **So even in a place where you'd think water is never going to be a problem, well guess what – even if we have water coming out of our ears I can't get it to anybody's house if I don't have electricity to pump it.**
>
> – Michael Jordan, COO, Metro regional government, Portland, Oregon (former City Manager, Canby, Oregon).

• **Levels of impact.** With this approach you focus on an issue, such as "emergency health care," and a general scenario, such as "significantly higher oil prices within the next few years." Then within that scenario, you list the things in your issue of focus that would be most immediately affected, and then think through how those first-level effects would cascade down to second, third and further levels.

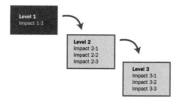

For example, taking "emergency health care" as your topic, you might identify:

• First-level impacts on transportation costs, which then create...

• Second-level impacts on transport of patients, commuting costs of medical specialists, and delivery of materials, which then create...

• Third-level impacts on timely treatment of patients, ability to retain medical specialists at remote institutions, costs of providing care, and so on...

Categorizing

Toward the end of your inquiry and initial analyses, you will have a big list of potential vulnerabilities covering many different kinds of issues and functions. Even if you had researched impacts by sector, department, or some other division, you may decide to categorize (or add a layer of categorization on to) these vulnerabilities for final analyses and later discussions for possible responses.

The right set of categories can be particularly useful for delineating who will be responsible for developing and implementing responses to these vulnerabilities. For example, you may combine vulnerabilities from "Transportation", "Food" and "Emergency Services" and recategorize them primarily as "local issues," "regional issues," and "national issues," or "short-term," "medium-term" and "long-term." A good practice from the risk assessment field is to categorize risks by the way in which they will ultimately be addressed (for example, by the responsible department).

Ranking

As you develop the picture of potential impacts and vulnerabilities, you'll recognize that some are more probable than others, and some are potentially more serious than others. A common approach for ranking risks is to identify both the potential effect (magnitude) and likelihood (probability) of each risk.

The Portland Peak Oil Task Force sub-group on transportation and land use used this method, starting with a list of potential impacts:

1) There will be an increase in car sharing and carpooling.
2) There will be a reduced demand for parking, freeing up land for other uses.
3) There will be an increased demand for compressed work week, telecommuting, etc.
4) There will be shorter, fewer car trips.
etc.

They then ranked these potential impacts in a matrix by likelihood of occurrence and potential magnitude of effect:

LIKELIHOOD	EFFECT		
	Major	Significant	Minor
High	4, 5, 10	2, 14, 18, 20	1, 7
50-50	9, 19	16	3, 8, 17
Low	15	6, 13	11, 12

Thus the committee felt that impact #3, "There will be an increased demand for compressed work week, telecommuting, etc.," had a 50-50 chance of happening, but would have a minor impact on the city. In contrast they felt that impact #4, "There will be shorter, fewer car trips," both highly probably and would have a major impact on the city (i.e., in the local economy).

Ranking can be a useful way to sort through a large number of ideas from a brainstorm to pick out the most significant issues. It can also be helpful for identifying the kinds of impacts that may call for further inquiry, perhaps with a scenario approach or level-of-impact approach as above.

Developing Conclusions

Once you've identified and ranked your community's vulnerabilities, develop responses to these vulnerabilities as action points for the community and the local government. Don't get sidetracked: refer back to the task force's initial charge, and develop your responses to address the original problem statement. Also, be sure to keep the big picture in mind. Don't develop a recommendation that makes sense for one particular sector or application, only to find that it would be premature, ineffective or even counterproductive from a broader system perspective.

Below are four guidelines for developing useful responses to you community's peak oil vulnerabilities. You will also find ideas in following the "five principles" for local government responses to energy and climate change listed in *Section 5.3 What your city can do*.

1. Start simple

When the Willits (California) Energy Committee was discussing energy vulnerability responses for their first recommendations to City Council, they set a guideline to only consider options that were proven and immediately available: no relying on future technological developments, no complicated strategies, no overly expensive investments.

Energy consultants often advise clients to first find energy cost savings with the "low-hanging fruit." This often means doing relatively easy energy efficiency initiatives, but it can also mean looking through existing policies and programs for relatively easy adjustments that, collectively, will significantly reduce overall peak oil vulnerability. With creative approaches, such as allocating funds saved through new efficiencies to investments in more efficient technologies, easy initial steps can produce big returns over the long term.

2. Keep it appropriate

The recommendations of your task force need to be appropriate for the people who will be acting on them. Focus on recommendations that move specific processes forward, rather than broad mandates that require significant organizational and political momentum.

For example, a recommendation like "Build an inter-city rail system for the region" is not very useful on its own, as such big decisions are made through complex processes of regional transportation planning and investment that take decades, and involve thousands of stakeholders across multiple jurisdictions. A more process-oriented recommendation like, "Study the feasibility of developing high-quality public transit service that connects cities in the region," would likely be more useful.

3. Keep it broad

A short-term initiative that encourages people to drive less is a good, basic response to energy uncertainty: it spurs people to consciously reduce their dependence on oil. A long-term policy that encourages urban development in transit-friendly regional centers, and less development in outlying rural areas, is a better response: it creates land use patterns that make it easy for people to reduce their dependence on oil while also protecting regional farmland. Avoid "silo" and quick fix solutions, and instead develop broad responses that cross issues and share resources. Comprehensive sustainability planning frameworks like The Natural Step[67] are excellent tools for this.

You may also be able to achieve a broad effect by initiating a specific action that touches off a chain of events. For example, a new policy like, "The City requires all transportation planning activities to consider future oil/gasoline price volatility as a key factor" would effectively engage a whole set of professional managers, planners, and engineers on the problem, with results that will go far beyond anything a time-limited task force could do.

Finally, a broad response also plans for ongoing uncertainty and assumes that changes will occur over time, taking a page from "adaptive management" practices. Don't plan specifics too far ahead or make unfounded assumptions, otherwise the decisions you recommend this year may unwittingly constrain your options for dealing with next year's situation.

4. Seek out examples and experts

There is no lack of examples throughout the world of communities that are thriving economically while minimizing their dependence on oil and natural gas. For example, hundreds of European cities of all sizes have implemented energy-smart policies and initiatives in the last fifty years, many of which are easily transferable to U.S. and Canadian cities.

In many cases, just by asking questions and being curious, you force people to re-look at what they've done. With our senior staff sometimes when I probe on issues, they'll sort of shrug at the end of it and say 'You know, I don't know why we do it that way! We've always done it that way.'

You've got to go in and change the way your bureaucrats think. Once you've got them changing the way they're thinking, it becomes much easier for your whole municipality to respond positively to the challenges that we're going to be facing.

- Mayor Derek Corrigan, City of Burnaby, British Columbia

Appendix

Cities in other parts of the world are pursuing urban sustainability as well, and often in extremely creative and low-cost ways. For example, the modern commercial center of Curitiba, Brazil (pop. ~1.65 million) has been lauded as "the most innovative city in the world" thanks to its unconventional and highly successful public transit, pedestrian mall, recycling, small business incubation, and flood control projects.

Presenting your findings, and cycling back

The way you present your task force findings will depend on the task force's charge, its audience, the urgency of its recommendations and other factors.

For example, the task forces in Portland and Sebastopol both developed sets of recommendations for their respective City Councils. The Portland task force identified eleven major recommendations (see *Box 7,* page 43), accompanied by recommended action items. In comparison, the Sebastopol task force (see *Box 8,* page 48) made 66 individual recommendations across nine different sectors (such as "Vehicles," "Water," and "City Revenues"), and then grouped them in summary as five "first steps," eight "implementation steps," and four steps for "making broader connections." Both task force reports described the vulnerabilities and impacts they identified.

As part of your task force recommendations you might include an item for reporting and follow-up, both to ensure that recommendations are acted upon and to adjust recommendations as needed. This is a good management practice for any program, but it's essential for dealing with energy uncertainty: if recommendations are not adjustable, then they may eventually be locked on to solutions for problems that have changed. Keep in mind that as the situation changes, the available options and the ability to forecast change as well.

Systems Thinking: A Tool for Municipalities

by Stephan E. Brown, M.A., and Daniel C. Lerch

Folks who do systems analysis have a great belief in 'leverage points.' These are places within a complex system (a corporation, an economy, a living body, a city, an ecosystem) where a small shift in one thing can produce big changes in everything....

...I don't think there are cheap tickets to system change. You have to work at it, whether that means rigorously analyzing a system or rigorously casting off paradigms. In the end, it seems that leverage has less to do with pushing levers than it does with disciplined thinking combined with strategically, profoundly, madly letting go.

> —Donella Meadows, lead author, *Limits to Growth* (1972). From "Places to Intervene in a System," *Whole Earth,* Winter 1997.

Systems theory has been put to practical use in the business world for decades, helping organize global production processes and streamline multinational decision-making networks. More recently, systems thinking concepts have been incorporated into a number of strategic planning methods for local governments.[a] These and other tools can help municipalities better understand the complex systems that are within them, and of which they are parts. Systems thinking will also help municipalities to understand the role of key inputs like oil and natural gas and to identify how municipalities are vulnerable to changes in the availability and price of those inputs.

What is Systems Thinking?

"Don't miss the forest for the trees." This common figure of speech encapsulates the essence of systems thinking: when we think in terms of systems, all we're doing is looking at the whole forest, and not just the trees.

What exactly do we see when we look at a forest? We see trees, certainly, but also animals, brush, soil, water, and many other things. If we put a bunch of trees, a pile of dirt, a tub of water and a family of squirrels together in a big room, however, we clearly wouldn't have a forest: we'd have a mess (or a bad art project). What makes a true forest are the *relationships* between all of its parts: the soil and water nourish the trees, the trees shelter the animals, the animals eat the plants, and so on.

So, systems thinking is first and foremost about relationships. And when we think about how the parts of a system relate to each other, we also notice *changes*: as the soil nourishes the trees, the trees grow larger; when animals and plants die, they decompose and build up more soil. By observing the relationships and changes in a system, we start to develop a comprehensive picture of how the system works. It also spurs us to ask important questions that may help us understand the system better: What happens to the animals and soil as the trees get bigger, and eventually die? What happens to the trees as the soil and animals change?

This way of thinking can be very helpful for understanding why things work (and change) the way they do. It can be applied to anything that is a system—a collection of individual parts working together—whether it's a forest, a car, or a government program. It's useful because if we understand how complex things change, and *why*, we can make better decisions to direct those changes as we see fit.

For example, 60 years ago we tried to stop forest fires as quickly as possible because we thought that fires were simply destroying trees. Since then we've learned that fires are an important part of forest systems, helping kill destructive insects, spread certain seeds, and reduce deadwood that could fuel even more disastrous future fires. Today we contain some fires and let others burn, and manage our healthier forests simultaneously for timber products, wildlife habitat, clean water and recreation. The better we understand the complex relationships in the forest system, the better we are at managing them.

When we do systems thinking, we are thinking about changes (or what systems thinkers call "dynamics") in terms of the relationships underlying them. Systems thinking thus views problems as the products of some structure of relationships, in contrast to conventional linear thinking, which instead explains patterns in terms of simple causes and effects between separate things.

The Municipality as a System

Just about everything that your municipality does or is responsible for can be thought of as a set of relationships, and therefore as a system. For example, your town's budgetary process can be thought of as a system of relationships between incoming tax revenue, the expenses of municipal departments, the priorities of elected officials, and the services the municipality provides. Similarly, your town's street program can be thought of as a system of relation-

Appendix

ships between the needs of the local economy, the municipal Transportation Plan, the costs of street construction and maintenance, and the city's street maintenance activities.

We can visualize these relationships in a flowchart (Figure A-1). The flowchart below shows that the Municipal Transportation Plan is derived from the needs of the local economy and the costs of building and maintaining streets; the Transportation Plan then affects what will happen with the street maintenance activities. Street construction costs can change quickly, however, so these are also shown as influencing street maintenance activities. Compare all the information this flowchart tells us with the simple list we might have produced had we thought of the street program simply in terms of its components, and not its relationships (Figure A-2).

- Transportation Plan
- Traffic Signals
- Asphalt
- Concrete
- Fill
- Work Crews

Figure A-1: Flowchart of Some Key Relationships that Characterize the Municipal Street Program

Figure A-2: List of Some Key Components of the Municipal Street Program

Both of these representations are incomplete pictures, of course, but the flowchart contains more information and suggests additional questions we can ask to gain a more complete picture. Looking at this diagram, we might next say: "Well, what influences the costs of street construction? What happens when the streets are (or aren't) maintained?" With systems thinking, we keep asking questions and revising our picture until we have a model of a system that makes sense to us and tells us what we want to know. For example, after a few rounds of additions and revisions we may end up with a revised flowchart like this:

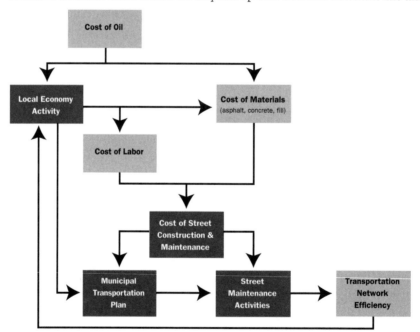

Figure A-3. Flowchart of Some Key Relationships that Characterize the Municipal Street Program (revised)

Asking about the costs of street construction got us thinking about the costs of materials and labor. The cost of labor is largely determined by the local economy, and one of the main material costs of street construction is asphalt, which is produced from oil, so we added these relationships to the picture. We also started to see additional relationships, such as the effect of street paving on transportation network efficiency, which in turn affects the local economy.

This flowchart is rather limited compared to true systems modeling techniques, but it demonstrates one of the main benefits of systems thinking: it gives us tools for identifying and exploring complex relationships. For example, if we developed this flowchart such that we could assign quantitative values to its elements, we could try changing certain variables to see how those changes ripple throughout the entire system. Or, we could use different techniques to identify weaknesses and trigger points, or test ways of improving the system's resilience to change.

Understanding Systems

Definition of a system

What is a system? All systems have two defining characteristics[b]: First, a system is made up of *component elements*, or **subsystems**, that are all related to each other in some way. Second, a system has a *structure*, or **metasystem**, that determines how these elements relate to each other.

Looking at Figure A-3, the street program flowchart, this definition tells us that (a) individual elements like "Cost of Labor" or "Transportation Network Efficiency" can be thought of as systems in their own right, and (b) the relationships between these individual elements are all part of a larger structure.

Boundaries

Whether we call something a "subsystem" or a "system" depends on our level of focus: a forest can be a system of trees, animals and streams, or it can be a subsystem of a larger ecological region. The level of focus we choose also determines the **boundary** of our system.

When we draw a system boundary, we're basically identifying which system elements are interacting with each other to produce the pattern of behavior that we're interested in explaining. The elements that receive inputs sit inside the boundary, and the elements that only provide inputs—but do not receive inputs themselves—are outside the boundary.[c] If we drew a boundary around our flowchart in Figure A-3, it would include everything except "Cost of Oil".

Choosing the right level of focus and boundary is important because if we're not clear about these things, we might not include relevant elements (or mistakenly include irrelevant ones) in our system and end up with a bad analysis—and then bad policy.

Feedback Loops

In systems thinking we differentiate between "simple" systems and "complex" systems. In simple systems, the chain of causes and effects between elements has a stopping point. Our first simple flowchart (Figure A-1), for example, would have been a simple system because it ended with "Street Maintenance Activities".

In a complex system, however, the chain of causes and effects doesn't have a stopping point—it becomes a **feedback loop**. Technically speaking, a feedback loop is a circular connection between two or more system elements in which a change in one element, or *input*, causes other elements to generate a response, or *output*, that eventually feeds back to the original element. In our more complex flowchart (Figure A-3), you can see a feedback loop flowing through the following variables:

    Local Economic Activity

        → Municipal Transportation Plan

            → Street Maintenance Activities

                → Transportation Network Efficiency

                    → Local Economic Activity

There are actually four distinct feedback loops in this figure—all starting and ending with "Local Economic Activity," but taking different paths through "Cost of Labor," "Cost of Materials" and "Cost of Street Construction and Maintenance."

Feedback loops can be either positive ("reinforcing") or negative ("balancing"). In a *positive* feedback loop, a change in one element will trigger changes that amplify, or reinforce, the original change. In a *negative* feedback loop, a change in one element will trigger changes that dampen, or balance, the original change. For example, if the feedback loop we described above is a positive loop, we could then say that the effects of a decrease in local economic activity would eventually result in *further* decreases in local economic activity.

Systems thinking gives us tools for identifying and exploring complex relationships.

If we don't choose the right boundary we may end up with bad analysis – and then bad policy.

Appendix

Leverage points are opportunities for changing system behavior with relatively little effort.

Parameters and Leverage Points

Systems are also composed of **parameters**. A parameter is a constant factor of a process, for example, a fractional change rate such as "productivity," "fertility," or "depreciation." In systems, *time delays* are important parameters. A time delay is the time it takes for a particular element to respond to an input. Time delays can significantly impact how systems behave, sometimes even making the difference between system success and failure.

By saying that parameters are "constant" factors, we mean that they are constant with respect to a given level of system complexity. However, at a higher (more complex) level, parameters can, themselves, be variable; that is, parameters can have parameters of their own. For example, in our municipality's street maintenance program, the productivity of road paving may be constant up to a certain level of activity, and then suddenly increase beyond that level by the introduction of efficiencies of scale.

When we build a model of a system, we ultimately want to identify the key parameters and the parts of its structure that seem to significantly influence the system's overall behavior. These important parts are called **leverage points** because they represent opportunities for changing system behavior with relatively little effort. When we adjust a leverage point we generally make a small change to certain parameters or relationships impacting some reinforcing feedback loop(s); in doing so, we take advantage of that loop's reinforcing cycle to create a large effect in the larger system.

For example, if road paving productivity is a critical limiting factor on system performance and is itself coupled to other factors in a positive (reinforcing) feedback loop, then a change in productivity or one of its inputs could trigger a "virtuous cycle" of improvement in system performance. In this case, productivity (or an input to it) is the leverage point we would want to target.

Dynamic equilibrium, resilience and uncertainty

A particularly important system pattern is called **dynamic equilibrium** (or "steady state" equilibrium). Think of the typical household heating system that regulates room temperature using a thermostat and heater. Figure A-4 represents temperature change in a house.

Here, the vertical axis represents the house temperature, measured in degrees Fahrenheit, while the horizontal axis represents time, measured in hours. The behavior pattern above is called an *oscillation pattern* because the system fluctuates around a set point: in this case, 68 degrees F.

System thinkers call this pattern a "goal-seeking" behavior because it appears as if the system is continuously comparing its actual state to some "goal" state, and then adjusting itself to narrow the gap between the two. The entire system is governed by a *negative feedback loop* that operates with some time delay; it's this time delay that generates the oscillating pattern. This dynamic equilibrium pattern may seem inefficient, but it actually reflects **system resilience**.

Healthy systems are resilient against uncertainty. In systems thinking, the concepts of *resilience* and *uncertainty* start with the idea that any system faces some risk of disruption whenever it is confronted with a change it doesn't expect and for which it has no appropriate response. "Uncertainty" can be thought of as the amount of surprise the environ-

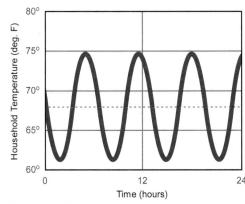

Figure A-4: Household temperature in dynamic equilibrium

ment represents to a given system. It follows from this that the persistence over time of a pattern of behavior represents a *reduction in uncertainty* between a system and its environment.[d] "Resilience", on the other hand, is the capacity or flexibility of a system to respond to changing environmental inputs in a consistent manner.[e] In the example above, the household heating system demonstrates resilience against the uncertainty of outside temperature by creating an "artificial" environment (or "bounded uncertainty") it can in a sense predict and therefore control.

Learning and "satisficing"

Systems can also adapt to deal with changing environments. This system adaptation process is called "learning," which can be thought of as any process that promotes resilience by reducing uncertainty. For example, natural forest fires play an important role in some forest ecosystems by regulating forest undergrowth to prevent cataclysmic fires. We could say that a forest ecosystem like this has "learned" to deal with the potentially catastrophic threat of fire by having structured itself in such a way that fires only clear the undergrowth that has accumulated since the last fire, and therefore do not burn hot or long enough to kill mature trees. The forest ecosystem is therefore more resilient because its "learned" structure reduces the uncertainty posed by fire.

That structure, as you may remember from our original definition of a "system," is called the *metasystem*. A metasystem lends resilience by systematically changing its system in such a way as to produce a controlled environmental disturbance. Each time the system "overshoots the goal," it produces an error (called a "steady state error") that it then responds to. By producing its own errors, the (meta)system can anticipate them, effectively reducing uncertainty. This strategy by which a smaller problem is generated so as to head off a more serious problem is called "error-controlled regulation" or "satisficing," and is common in biological and even social systems dealing with complex and turbulent environments.[f]

Learning is a form of adaptation, but it can also be addictive. Have you worked with someone who ritualistically creates their own crisis because they prefer a familiar problem to the totally unfamiliar? Or consider the adage, "When the only tool you have is a hammer, every problem begins to resemble a nail"; we similarly tend to perceive only those types of problems for which we have a solution. So long as a particular arrangement functions, this "addiction" of creating problems to solve is not necessarily a problem. But we all know how difficult it can be to change a habit after the environment changes, even if it is plain to us that the habit no longer serves us. In such cases, we may end up treating the symptoms instead of the cause[g]. Systems thinking gives us a way of understanding both learning and the roots of resistance to learning: the two are deeply related.

Because any change requires an expenditure of resources, learning follows an "economy of flexibility" in which the capacity to adapt is purchased at the price of habit formation.[h] Alternatively, we can think of error—within an allowable range of tolerance, anyway—as the price we pay for our (always limited) capacity to respond to multiple environmental demands[i]. This trade-off applies to all kinds of learning, including the learning that ideally occurs in planning and policymaking. When we make municipal plans and policies, we act as "satisficing" metasystems learning about the urban system we are attempting to regulate.

Modeling

These basic concepts provide only a brief introduction to systems thinking, but they are also useful tools in themselves for understanding complexity and change. The next step is to learn about modeling, which gives us a way of deriving practical lessons from an otherwise abstract picture of a system.

Systems thinking is fundamentally a decision-making process by which we create models of system behaviors, and then test them to understand the system better. We can use models to explain the causes of a system problem, and then develop solutions that will withstand the range of expected conditions. For example, using a model of a municipal system, we could propose various municipal policies by changing the structures or parameters that have been identified as leverage points and then proceed to test these policy solutions under different hypothetical conditions. Stakeholder-based or collaborative modeling can play a valuable role in policy "learning," starting with problem scoping or definition. Indeed, since much of municipal complexity arises from the diversity of experiences and perspectives, modeling should include stakeholders in the process as much as possible.[j]

Resources for Practical Applications

Systems thinking is still a relatively new tool for municipal policy and urban planning, but it holds great promise for managing complex problems such as energy and climate uncertainty. The resources listed below will help you further explore the practical applications of this exciting field.

Pegasus Communications (www.thesystemsthinker.com)

Pegasus is a leading provider of practical resources on systems thinking, management innovation, organizational change, and the next-generation workplace. Publisher of "The Systems Thinker" newsletter, a highly-accessible print and online resource for learning about systems thinking.

The Natural Step (www. naturalstep.com)

The Natural Step is a framework grounded in natural science that serves as a guide for businesses, communities, educators, government entities, and individuals on the path toward sustainable development. Developed in Sweden in 1988, The Natural Step framework encourages dialogue, consensus building, and systems thinking and creates the conditions for profound change to occur.

When we make municipal plans and policies, we act as "satisficing" metasystems learning about the urban system we are attempting to regulate.

Appendix

Eco-municipalities (www.sjamesassociates.com; www.sekom.nu)
A quarter of all municipalities in Sweden have adopted the Natural Step framework as guiding policy. Known as eco-municipalities (*"ekokommuner"*), these jurisdictions have started a movement that has recently spread to the United States. Sarah James Associates (www.sjamesassociates.com) provides consultation and resources on pursuing the eco-municipality idea in the United States.

Resilience Alliance (www.resalliance.org)
The Resilience Alliance is a research organization comprised of scientists and practitioners from many disciplines who collaborate to explore the dynamics of social-ecological systems. The Resilience Alliance website includes an active discussion area and resource databases that occasionally touch on urban issues.

Works Cited and Suggested Readings

Ashby, W.R. (1956). *An introduction to cybernetics.* London: Methuen & Co. Ltd.

Bateson, G. (1979). *Mind and nature: A necessary unity.* New York: Bantam.

Checkland, P. and Scholes, J. (1990). *Soft systems methodology.* New York: Wiley.

Innes, J.E. & Booher, D.E. (1999). Consensus building and complex adaptive systems: a framework for evaluating collaborative planning. *Journal of the American Planning Association,* 65(4), 412-23.

Khisty, C.J. (1995). Soft-systems methodology as learning and management tool. *Journal of Urban Planning and Development,* 121(3), 91-107.

Lendaris, G.G. (1986). On systemness and the problem solver: tutorial comments, *IEEE,* SMC-16(4).

Linstone, H.A. (1999). *Decision making for technology executives: Using multiple perspectives to improve performance.* Boston: Artech House.

Mostashari, A. & Sussman, J. (2005). Stakeholder-assisted modeling and policy design process for environmental decision-making. J*ournal of Environmental Assessment Policy & Management,* 7(3) 355-386.

Presley, A. & Meade, L. (2002). The role of soft systems methodology in planning for sustainable production. *GMI,* 37, 101-110.

Purnomo, H., Mendoza, G.A., & Prabhu, R. (2004). Model for collaborative planning of community-managed resources based on qualitative soft systems approach. *Journal of Tropical Forest Science,* 16(1), 106-31.

Richmond, B. (2001). *An introduction to systems thinking, STELLA.* High Performance Systems, Inc.

Senge, P.M. (1990). *The fifth discipline: The art and practice of the learning organization.* 1st ed. New York: Doubleday.

Seymoar, N.-K. (2004) *Planning for Long-term Urban Sustainability: A Guide to Frameworks and Tools.* Vancouver, BC: +30 Network.

Shannon, C.E. & Weaver, W. (1975). *The mathematical theory of information.* Urbana, Ill: University of Illinois Press (first published 1949).

Simon, H.A. (1996). *The sciences of the artificial.* Cambridge, Mass: MIT Press.

Sterman, J.D. (2000). *Business dynamics: Systems thinking and modeling for a complex world.* Boston: Irwin McGraw-Hill.

Van den Belt, M. (2004). *Mediated modeling: A system dynamics approach to environmental consensus building.* Washington, D.C.: Island Press.

Walker, B., Gunderson, L., Kinzig, A., Folke, C., Carpenter, S., & Schultz, L. (2006). A handful of heuristics and some propositions for understanding resilience in socio-ecological systems. *Ecology and Society,* 11(1), 13.
Online: http://www.ecologyandsociety.org/vol11/iss1/art13/.

Endnotes

a. Seymoar, N.-K., 2004.

b. cf. Lendaris, 1986.

c. Sterman, 2000.

d. Shannon & Weaver, 1975.

e. Walker et al., 2006.

f. Ashby, 1956; Simon, 1996.

g. Senge, 1990.

h. Bateson, 1979.

i. Simon, 1996.

j. Innes & Booher, 1999; Linstone, 1999; Mendoza & Sussman, 2005; Purnomo et al., 2004.

Post Carbon Cities: Planning for Energy and Climate Uncertainty

Resources

Post Carbon Cities website

Visit the companion website to this Guidebook, www.postcarboncities.net, for the latest news, discussion and resources on addressing energy and climate change from the local government level. The website includes:

- News from around the world on how cities are addressing the challenges of energy and climate uncertainty.
- Special Features by leading professionals, scholars and elected officials, developed exclusively for Post Carbon Cities and Post Carbon Institute.
- A Resource Database of policy tools, reports, case studies and best practices.

Peak oil reports by and for local government

Charting a Path for a New Energy Future for Sebastopol (2007)
By Sebastopol (California) Citizens Advisory Group on Energy Vulnerability for Sebastopol City Council.
http://www.postcarboncities.net/node/134

Descending the Oil Peak: Navigating the Transition from Oil and Natural Gas (2007)
By Portland (Oregon) Peak Oil Task Force for Portland City Council.
http://www.portlandonline.com/osd/index.cfm?c = 42894&

Global Peak in Oil Production: The Municipal Context (2006)
By City of Burnaby (British Columbia) Transportation Committee.
http://www.postcarboncities.net/node/164

Hamilton: The Electric City (2006)
By Richard Gilbert for City of Hamilton (Ontario) City Council.
http://www.postcarboncities.net/node/267

Recommendations towards Energy Independence for the City of Willits and Surrounding Community (2005)
By Willits (California) Economic Localization and Willits Ad Hoc Energy Group for City of Willits.
http://www.willitseconomiclocalization.org/Archives/PreparedPapers

Guidebooks

Energy and Planning

U.S. Mayors' Climate Action Handbook (2006)
By ICLEI-Local Governments for Sustainability, the City of Seattle and the U.S. Conference of Mayors.
This concise handbook is a resource for implementing actions under the U.S. Mayors' Climate Protection Agreement. It includes sample actions, tools and best practices and resources on topics such as land use, energy efficiency, water management and waste reduction.
http://www.iclei.org/documents/USA/documents/CCP/Climate_Action_Handbook-0906.pdf

California Local Energy Efficiency Program Workbook (2006)
By Navigant Consulting for California Local Energy Efficiency Program / California Public Utilities Commission.
The CALeep Workbook lays out a process for instituting local energy efficiency programs. It is a tool to be used by local officials and community activists to initiate, plan, organize, implement, and assess energy efficiency activities at the local and regional level. Communities can follow this process to increase their level of energy efficiency, whether starting from scratch or building on existing energy efficiency activities.
http://www.caleep.com/workbook/workbook.htm

Saving Oil in a Hurry: Measures for Rapid Demand Restraint in Transport (2005)
By International Energy Agency, Paris.
This book provides a new, quantitative assessment of the potential oil savings and costs of rapid oil demand restraint measures for transport. Some measures may make sense under any circumstances; others are primarily useful in emergency situations. All can be implemented on short notice—if governments are prepared. The book examines potential approaches for rapid uptake of telecommuting, "ecodriving", and car-pooling, among other measures. It also provides methodologies and data that policymakers can use to decide which measures would be best adapted to their national circumstances.
http://www.postcarboncities.net/node/425

Appendix

Sustainable Energy: Power Solutions for Local Governments (2001)
By International City/County Management Association, Washington, DC. IQ Report 33:4.
This report establishes a context in which to examine renewable energy resources and suggests a wide range of strategies for modernizing local government energy systems. It discusses how local governments can use renewable energy (i.e., solar, wind, small hydro, bioenergy, and geothermal power), addresses program development, and outlines ways to get citizens to support municipal energy projects. The report concludes with a list of resource organizations and selected readings.
http://bookstore.icma.org

The Energy Yardstick: Using PLACE³S to Create More Sustainable Communities (1996)
By California Energy Commission, Oregon Department of Energy and Washington State Energy Office.
PLACE³S ("PLAnning for Community Energy, Economic and Environmental Sustainability") is a land use and urban design method that uses energy as a yardstick to help communities understand how their growth and development decisions can contribute to improved sustainability. This book describes the method in detail and provides case studies of projects where it has been used. The project website includes updates with new case studies and documentation.
http://www.energy.ca.gov/places/index.html

Land Use Planning

Planning for long-term urban sustainability: A guide to frameworks and tools (2004)
By PLUS Network (formerly 30+ Network), Vancouver, British Columbia.
This guide reviews eight different systems-oriented comprehensive planning frameworks used by cities around the world, including The Natural Step, the Sheltair Adaptive Management Framework and ICLEI's Local Agenda 21 frameworks.
http://www.sustainablecommunities.fcm.ca/Tools

Getting to Smart Growth: 100 Policies for Implementation (2002)
By Smart Growth Network (SGN) and the International City/County Management Association (ICMA).
This primer serves as a roadmap for states and communities that have recognized the need for smart growth, but are unclear on how to achieve it. SGN and ICMA released the follow-up *Getting to Smart Growth II: 100 More Policies for Implementation* in 2003.
http://www.smartgrowth.org

Growing Smart Legislative Guidebook and User Manual: Model Statutes for Planning and the Management of Change (2002)
By the American Planning Association.
This two-volume Guidebook is the culmination of APA's seven-year Growing Smart project, an effort to draft the next generation of model planning and zoning legislation for the U.S. The User Manual helps those interested in statutory reform navigate through the Guidebook and, by means of checklists and case studies, select from the options available in the Guidebook and tailor a program of statutory reform that will meet the unique needs of their state.
http://www.planning.org/growingsmart

The Smart Growth Toolkit: helping to create more livable communities in British Columbia (2001)
By Smart Growth BC, Vancouver, British Columbia.
This toolkit provides an overview of smart growth, smart growth tools, citizen involvement strategies and references on additional information sources.
http://www.smartgrowth.bc.ca

Support Organizations

Energy Efficiency and Renewable Energy
American Council for an Energy-Efficient Economy (ACEEE)
http://www.aceee.org
ACEEE provides research, policy analysis, conferences and education on energy efficiency as a means of promoting both economic prosperity and environmental protection. Collaborating with experts from universities, national laboratories, and the private sector, ACEEE has helped develop efficiency programs and policies for utilities, states and the federal government. They also provide technical assistance and research on energy efficiency in building, industrial applications, agriculture and transportation.

Database of State Incentives for Renewable Energy (DSIRE)
http://www.dsireusa.org
DSIRE is a regularly updated database of state, local, utility, and selected federal incentives

that promote energy efficiency and renewable energy. DSIRE is funded by the U.S. Department of Energy and managed by the North Carolina State University's College of Engineering.

National Association of Energy Service Companies (NAESCO)
http://www.naesco.org
NAESCO publishes case studies focused on energy efficiency retrofits in local government facilities in the United States. These case studies demonstrate that local governments can modernize schools, hospitals, and municipal infrastructure and, at the same time, reduce operating costs.

Natural Resources Canada—Office of Energy Efficiency (OEE)
http://oee.nrcan.gc.ca/communities-government
OEE provides information on federal programs available for helping municipalities and commercial enterprises achieve greater energy efficiencies in building management, fleet management, procurement and other areas. Its larger program promotes efficiency and alternative fuels for the residential, commercial, industrial and transportation sectors. OEE publishes the annual "State of Energy Efficiency in Canada."

United States Department of Energy, State Energy Program
http://www.eere.energy.gov/state_energy_program
The State Energy Program (SEP) provides grants to states and directs funding to state energy offices from technology programs in DOE's Office of Energy Efficiency and Renewable Energy. States use grants to address their energy priorities and program funding to adopt emerging renewable energy and energy efficiency technologies.

Renewable Energy Policy Project (REPP)
http://www.repp.org
REPP's goal is to accelerate the use of renewable energy by providing credible information, insightful policy analysis, and innovative strategies amid changing energy markets and mounting environmental needs. REPP's activities include researching, publishing, and disseminating information, creating policy tools, and hosting on-line renewable energy discussion groups.

Governance—Canada
Canadian Association of Municipal Administrators (CAMA/ACAM)
http://www.camacam.ca
CAMA is a national, non-profit association of municipal managers and executives that provides professional development and a national forum for municipal management.

Federation of Canadian Municipalities (FCM)
http://www.fcm.ca
FCM represents the interests of municipalities on policy and program matters that fall within federal jurisdiction. Members include Canada's largest cities, small urban and rural communities, and 18 provincial and territorial municipal associations. FCM promotes strong, effective and accountable municipal government, and also serves as a professional association for elected municipal officials.

Governance—International
International City/County Management Association
http://www.icma.org
ICMA advocates and develops the professional management of local government, providing publications, data, information, technical assistance, and training and professional development to thousands of city, town, and county experts and other individuals throughout the world. The organization is an internationally recognized publisher of information resources.

Governance—United States
National Association of Regional Councils (NARC)
http://www.narc.org
NARC is an association of regional councils, region-wide associations of local governments (i.e., "councils of government", or COGs), regional planning and development agencies and metropolitan planning organizations (MPOs). NARC represents and advocates for the interests of its members at the national level, and supports its members through trainings, technical assistance and networking opportunities.

National Association of Towns and Townships
http://www.natat.org
The National Association of Towns and Townships (NATaT) represents small U.S. communities—towns, townships and other suburban and rural localities—at the federal level. NATaT advocates for fair-share federal funding decisions and for legislative and regulatory policies to strengthen grassroots local government. In particular, NATaT seeks flexible and alternative approaches to federal policies to ensure that small communities can meet federal requirements.

Appendix

National League of Cities
http://www.nlc.org
The National League of Cities is the oldest and largest national organization representing municipal governments throughout the United States. Its mission is to strengthen and promote cities as centers of opportunity, leadership, and governance. Working in partnership with the 49 state municipal leagues, the League advocates for cities and towns in Washington, D.C. and provides programs and services for local leaders.

The Public Entity Risk Institute (PERI)
http://www.riskinstitute.org
PERI is a resource for enhancing the practice of risk management throughout organizations and communities. Serving public entities, small businesses, and nonprofit organizations, PERI provides enterprise risk management information, training, data, and data analysis.

United States Conference of Mayors (USCM)
http://www.usmayors.org
USCM is the official nonpartisan organization of cities with populations of 30,000 or more. The primary roles of The USCM are to promote the development of effective national urban/suburban policy, strengthen federal-city relationships, ensure that federal policy meets urban needs, provide mayors with leadership and management tools, and serve as a forum in which mayors can share ideas and information. USCM also publishes reports such as an annual Energy Best Practices Guide.

Sustainability and Climate

Business Alliance for Local Living Economies (BALLE)
http://www.livingeconomies.org
BALLE is 15,000-member strong meta-network of over 50 local business networks throughout the U.S. and Canada supporting the growth and development of community-based businesses. Members of local networks encourage local purchasing by consumers and businesses and advocate public policies that strengthen independent local businesses, promote economic equity, and protect the environment. BALLE connects its local networks to share best practices, and provides members with tools, business models, and other resources

FCM Centre for Sustainable Community Development
http://www.sustainablecommunities.fcm.ca
The Federation of Canadian Municipalities' Centre for Sustainable Community Development offers financial services and resources to Canadian municipal governments to improve environmental performance and reduce greenhouse gas emissions. The organization's mission is to demonstrate municipal leadership in sustainable community development by working with partners to implement holistic decision-making, planning processes and innovative projects. Major programs include the Green Municipal Fund and Partners for Climate Protection, through which FCM implements ICLEI's Cities for Climate Protection program in Canada.

ICLEI—Local Governments for Sustainability
http://www.iclei.org
ICLEI is an international association of local governments dedicated to preventing and solving local, regional, and global environmental problems through local action. Participation in ICLEI campaigns and regional projects provides local governments with technical tools, policy guidance, training, and technical expertise to advance climate protection and implement innovative solutions to environmental challenges. ICLEI's Cities for Climate Protection Campaign has worked with local governments around the world since 1993 to reduce greenhouse gas emissions through a comprehensive and strategic analysis and quantification approach.

C40 Climate Leadership Group
http://www.c40cities.org/solutions/casestudies
C40 is a group of the world's largest cities committed to tackling climate change. Originally a partnership between the international Large Cities Climate Leadership Group and the Clinton Climate Initiative, C40 works on the creation of procurement policies and alliances to accelerate the uptake of climate-friendly technologies and influence the global marketplace. The C40 website includes a database of city best practices.

Local Government Commission
http://www.lgc.org
The Local Government Commission (LGC) is a nonprofit, nonpartisan, membership organization providing resources and technical assistance specifically to local elected officials and other dedicated community leaders who are working to create healthy, walkable, and resource-efficient communities. Although focused on California communities, many of LGC's resources and services are applicable throughout the United States.

Local Government Environmental Assistance Network (LGEAN)

http://www.lgean.org

LGEAN serves local government officials, managers and staff in the United States. The LGEAN website includes news, webcasts, regulatory information, and a toolbox of resources. LGEAN is a program of the International City/County Management Association (ICMA) in partnership with the U.S Environmental Protection Agency (EPA) and eight national associations involved with local government and/or resource management.

Mayors for Climate Protection

http://www.coolmayors.com

Mayors for Climate Protection is the web portal for mayors to take action on climate change either through signing the US Mayors Climate Protection Agreement or joining ICLEI's Cities for Climate Protection Campaign. The website includes profiles of participating mayors and links to further resources for mayors and cities.

SustainLane Government

http://www.sustainlane.us

With over 300 participating cities, states and counties, SustainLane Government is a leading online sustainability best practices knowledge base for state and local government. SustainLane Government evolved from the SustainLane US City Rankings, a benchmark study on urban sustainability published in June 2005. Free to government professionals and their consultants, SustainLane Government also provides a searchable network of sustainability managers, experts and practitioners, enabling government entities, large and small, to work more efficiently toward sustainable policies and practices.

Urban Planning

Association of Metropolitan Planning Organizations (AMPO)

http://www.ampo.org

AMPO serves the needs and interests of metropolitan planning organizations (MPOs) nationwide by providing technical assistance and training, conferences, research, and a forum for transportation policy development and coalition building.

Planetizen

http://www.planetizen.com

Planetizen is a leading online forum for the urban planning, design, and development community. It includes urban planning news, commentary, interviews, event coverage, book reviews, announcements, jobs, consultant listings, training, and other resource. Content on Planetizen covers a wide number of planning, design, and development issues, from transportation to global warming, architecture to infrastructure, housing and community development to historic preservation.

Project for Public Spaces (PPS)

http://www.pps.org

PPS provides technical assistance, training, research and other services to create and sustain public spaces that build communities. Since 1975, PPS has worked in over 1,500 communities in the United States, Canada and around the world, helping people turn their public spaces into vital community places.

Smart Growth America

http://www.smartgrowthamerica.org

Smart Growth America is a coalition of nearly 100 state and national advocacy organizations that have a stake in how metropolitan expansion affects the environment, quality of life and economic sustainability. The diverse coalition partners include national, state and local groups working on behalf of the environment, historic preservation, social equity, land conservation, neighborhood redevelopment, farmland protection, labor, town planning, and more.

Smart Growth Canada Network (SGCN)

http://www.smartgrowth.ca

SCGN advances the implementation of smart growth and sustainability principles across Canada. SCGN provides networking opportunities and online courses.

Smart Growth Network

http://www.smartgrowth.org

Smart Growth Network raises awareness, promotes best practices and develops tools for smart growth. The Network's partners tend to work at a national level, and include environmental groups, historic preservation organizations, professional organizations, developers, real estate interests, and government entities.

Appendix

Urban Land Institute (ULI)
http://www.uli.org/
ULI is a nonprofit research and educational institute whose mission is to provide responsible leadership in the use of land in order to enhance the total environment. Established in 1936, the institute today has some 30,000 members and associates from fifty countries representing the entire spectrum of the land use and development disciplines. As the preeminent, multidisciplinary real estate forum, ULI facilitates the open exchange of ideas, information and experience among local, national and international industry leaders and policy makers dedicated to creating better places.

Energy news and data
Association for the Study of Peak Oil and Gas (ASPO)
http://www.aspo-usa.com; http://aspocanada.ca
ASPO is a global network of non-profit, independent organizations working to raise public awareness of oil and gas depletion and its consequences. ASPO's weekly newsletters and annual conference are among the best quality sources of news and critical analysis on the issues of peak oil and peak natural gas.

EnergyBulletin.net
http://www.energybulletin.net
EnergyBulletin.net is an independent clearinghouse for current information about the peaking of global energy supply and its implications and consequences. The editors publish news and opinion from a variety of viewpoints on energy resource supply and related issues like housing, transportation, agriculture, waste and local solutions.

International Energy Agency (IEA)
http://www.iea.org
The IEA acts as energy policy advisor to 26 member countries (all members of the Organization for Economic Co-operation and Development) in their efforts to ensure reliable, affordable and clean energy for their citizens. The IEA's initial role was to coordinate international measures in times of oil supply emergencies. Its work now also includes market reform, climate change policies, energy technology collaboration and outreach.

U.S. Energy Information Administration (EIA)
http://www.eia.doe.gov
The EIA is a statistical agency of the U.S. Department of Energy. It provides data, forecasts, and analyses to promote sound policy making, efficient markets, and public understanding regarding energy and its interaction with the economy and the environment.

Endnotes

1 Chevron began an unusual ad campaign in 2006 featuring messages like "The world consumes two barrels of oil for every barrel discovered. (So is this something you should be worried about?)" and "World energy demand could more than double in the next 50 years. (So where would we get the energy everyone needs?)" See Box 1, page 13.

2 Hirsch, Robert. et al. (2005) "Peaking of World Oil Production: Impacts, Mitigation, & Risk Management." Washington, D.C.: U.S. Department of Energy. Page 30.

3 Farrell, A. "Ethanol Demand Burns Meat Producers." Forbes, 9 March 2007.

4 A number of key factors seem to have brought this about, most notably: the Kyoto Protocol going into effect (without U.S. ratification) in February 2005; the devastation caused by Hurricane Katrina in September 2005; the success of former U.S. Vice President Al Gore's global warming film, "An Inconvenient Truth," released in May 2006; California's adoption of greenhouse gas emissions caps in August 2006; the release of the "Economics of Climate Change" report by U.K. economist Sir Edward Stern in October 2006; a shift among key U.S. conservative religious groups towards accepting the need to address global warming; U.S. President George W. Bush's acknowledgement of "the serious challenge of global climate change" in his State of the Union in January 2007; and the March 2007 release of the Fourth Assessment Report of the Intergovernmental Panel of Climate Change.

5 For a succinct overview of some potential catastrophic effects of global warming, see Gagosian, R. (2003) "Abrupt Climate Change: Should We Be Worried?" Woods Hole, MA: Woods Hole Oceanographic Institution.
Online at http://www.whoi.edu/institutes/occi/viewArticle.do?id=9986.

6 Leotta, K. Interview with author, 12 July 06. See also Leotta, K. (2006) "Fuel Price, Availability, and Mobility: What We Can Learn from North Carolina in the Aftermath of Hurricane Katrina." Seattle: Parsons Brinkerhoff.
Online at http://www.postcarboncities.net/node/73.

7 James Hansen, director of NASA's Goddard Institute for Space Studies, has set a timeline of ten years for making the changes necessary to keep global warming from reaching 2° Celsius over pre-industrial levels, warmer than the Earth has been in a million years. See Dr. Hansen's presentation at the February 2007 "2010 Imperative" international webcast design teach-in at www.2010imperative.org.

8 Skrebowski, C. Communication with author, 8 November 2006.

9 Skrebowski, C., op. cit.

10 The Organisation of Petroleum Exporting Countries (OPEC) coordinates the petroleum production and export policies of its members, which include Algeria, Indonesia, Iran, Iraq, Kuwait, Libya, Nigeria, Qatar, Saudi Arabia, the United Arab Emirates, and Venezuela. OPEC members produce about 40% of the world's oil.

11 The Organisation for Economic Co-operation and Development (OCED) is a group of 30 industrialized democracies including most European countries, the United States, Canada, Mexico, Japan, South Korea, Australia, New Zealand and Turkey.

12 Maidment, P. (2006, May 12) "Oil: It's all about supply." Forbes.

13 Skrebowski, C., op. cit.

14 Skrebowski, C., op. cit. Of 84m barrels per day of total oil production in 2005, non-conventional oil was 2m b/d, or 2.4%; this included 1m b/d of Canadian tar sands, 600,000 b/d of Venezuelan heavy oil, and around 400,000 b/d of biofuels. Non-conventional oil production is projected to increase to 6% of total oil production by 2015.

15 Royal Dutch Shell was sued by its shareholders in 2004 for allegedly overstating its oil and gas reserves by 20%. Mexico admitted in 2002 it had been overstating its reserves by over 50%.

16 Darley, J. (2004) High Noon for Natural Gas. White River Jct.: Chelsea Green.

17 Of course, oil and gas have their limitations as well. Oil has serious environmental hazards, including localized damage where it is drilled, the potential for damage if it is spilled in transport, and the carbon dioxide and other greenhouse gases it releases when it is burned. Natural gas is difficult to transport given the logistical challenges of transporting a highly flammable gas under pressure. Moreover, the drilling of oil and gas in many parts of the world is wrought with human rights problems, from local power conflicts to environmental devastation.

Appendix

18 EROI is the "ratio of the energy delivered by a process to the energy used directly and indirectly in that process". It is also known as EROEI ("energy returned on energy invested"), and "energy profit ratio," and is related to the concept of "net energy." (See Cleveland, C., Costanza, R. (2006) "Energy return on investment (EROI)." In C. J. Cleveland (Ed.) *Encyclopedia of Earth*. Washington, D.C.: National Council for Science and the Environment. Online at www.eoearth.org.)

19 EROI figures are from Cleveland, C. et al. (1984) "Energy and the U.S. Economy: A Biophysical Perspective," *Science*, 225:4665(890-897). Energy content figures are from Bioenergy Feedstock Information Network, Oak Ridge National Laboratory, U.S. Department of Energy; see http://bioenergy.ornl.gov/papers/misc/energy_conv.html.

20 Oil Shale and Tar Sands Leasing Programmatic EIS Information Center, U.S. Bureau of Land Management. http://ostseis.anl.gov/guide/tarsands/index.cfm, captured 12 Oct. 2006.

21 Zittel, W. and Schindler, J. (2007) "Coal: Resources and Future Production." Ottobrunn, Germany: Energy Watch Group.
Online at http://www.energywatchgroup.org/files/coalreport.pdf.

22 See also "Coal's Future in Doubt," a 9 May 2007 special update to peak oil researcher Richard Heinberg's monthly newsletter.
Online at http://globalpublicmedia.org/heinberg_coals_future_in_doubt.

23 Armistead, T. et al. (2006, September 18) "Nuclear power: New realities bring about a construction climate change." *Engineering News-Record*.

24 Zittel, W. and Schindler, J. (2006) "Uranium Resources and Nuclear Energy." Ottobrunn, Germany: Energy Watch Group. Available online at http://www.energywatchgroup.org/files/uraniumreport.pdf.

25 Ethanol's share of total corn use in the United States is expected to increase from 18% in 2006/07 to 26% in 2007/08. See U.S. Department of Agriculture, (2007) "Grains and Oilseeds Outlook for 2007," Agricultural Outlook Forum 2007, 2 March 2007.
Online at http://www.usda.gov/oce/forum/2007%20Speeches/index.htm.

26 Heilbrun, J. (1987). "The Economics of Urban Transportation." From *Urban Economics and Public Policy*, 3rd ed., p. 173-206. McGraw-Hill.

27 Dantas, A. et al. (2005) "Performance-Objective Design for Energy Constrained Transportation System." *Journal of the Eastern Asia Society for Transportation Studies*, v6 pp 3276-3292.

28 Small, K. (1980) "Energy Scarcity and Urban Development Patterns," International Regional Science Review, v5 n2 pp97-117; Evans, A. and Beed, C. (1986) "Transport Costs and Urban Property Values in the 1970s," Urban Studies, 1986:2, 105-117.

29 Such "district heating" and "combined heat and power" (CHP) systems are increasingly common in European cities; see International District Energy Association, www.districtenergy.org.

30 Local chapters of BALLE (Business Alliance for Local Living Economy), a growing network of locally-owned businesses in the U.S. and Canada, are relatively new resources of local business leaders interested in sustainability issues.

31 The Portland, Oregon metropolitan area MPO, "Metro" (www.metro-region.org), is the country's sole elected regional government.

32 Charton, S. (2004, 21 March) "Hayden now ready to embrace Buffalo Commons initiative." Associated Press.

33 Popper, F. Interview with author, 18 July 2006.

34 Popper, D. Interview with author, 21 July 2006.

35 Seymoar, N.-K. (2004) "Planning for Long-term Urban Sustainability: A Guide to Frameworks and Tools." Vancouver, BC: +30 Network.

36 The LUTRAQ ("Land Use, Transportation and Air Quality") model developed by 1000 Friends of Oregon (www.friends.org) to defeat the Western Bypass project has since been used in many other metropolitan areas.
See http://www.friends.org/resources/lut_reports.html.

37 Portland Peak Oil (www.portlandpeakoil.org) is a member of Post Carbon Institute's Relocalization Network (www.relocalize.net).

38 Metro (www.metro-region.org) is the regional government of the Portland metropolitan region; it is primarily responsible for coordinating long-range land use and transportation planning among its member municipalities. It also manages the region's urban growth boundary, solid waste and recycling system, regional visitors facilities such as a convention center and zoo, and a network of parks and greenspaces. Metro is the only elected regional government body in the United States.

39 City of Portland, Oregon. Council Resolution 36407, adopted 10 May 2006.

40 Interviews with Portland Peak Oil Task Force members, February 2007.

41 Armstrong, M. Correspondence with author, 13 June 2007.

42 John Kasara's "aerotropolis" concept consists of an airport city core and outlying corridors and clusters of aviation-linked businesses. See http://www.aerotropolis.com.

43 A 2005 policy paper (City of Hamilton, Ontario. January 2005. "Development of Policy Papers for Phase Two of the Transportation Master Plan for the City of Hamilton: Transportation Energy Use and Greenhouse Gas Emissions Policy Paper," page 13) underpinning the Transportation Master Plan noted that "a dramatic increase in fuel costs beginning before 2015 is very likely" as a result of peak oil. However, future energy constraints had not been seriously considered in 30-year plan according to City staff at a June 2005 public meeting (Santa Barbara, J. correspondence with the author 16 June 2007).

44 Santa Barbara, J. and McLean, D. (Hamiltonians for Progressive Development, correspondence with author, 16 June 2007; and, Citizens at City Hall, (2006, November 8), "Peak oil lost in city bureaucracy," Hamilton, Ontario (www.hamiltoncatch.org).

45 Peace, G. Interview with author, 2 Nov. 2006.

46 WELL (www.willitseconomiclocalization.org) is a member of Post Carbon Institute's Relocalization Network (www.relocalize.net).

47 Corzilius, B. Interview with author, 27 July 2006.

48 The Oil Depletion Protocol is an international agreement for nations of the world to cooperatively reduce their dependence on oil. It was proposed by Dr. Colin Campbell, a prominent petroleum geologist and founder of the Association for the Study of Peak Oil and Gas (ASPO), in 1996.

49 Post Carbon Institute's Relocalization Network (http://www.relocalize.net/) and the Oil Awareness section of the website Meetup.com (http://oilawareness.meetup.com/) are the two largest communication and resource networks of these citizen groups, many of which directly advocate for action on energy uncertainty by their local governments.

50 Donaghy, T. et al. (2007) "Atmosphere of Pressure: Political Interference in Federal Climate Science." Cambridge, MA: Union of Concerned Scientists. Available online at http://www.ucsusa.org/assets/documents/scientific_integrity/Atmosphere-of-Pressure.pdf

51 ICLEI was founded as International Council for Local Environmental Initiatives, but is now known as ICLEI-Local Governments for Sustainability. Their Cities for Climate Protection five-milestone framework is the largest program working with cities around the world to track and reduce local greenhouse gas emissions. In Canada, this program is implemented for ICLEI by the Federation of Canadian Municipalities as "Partners for Climate Change"; see http://www.iclei.org.

52 See http://www.usclimatenetwork.org and http://www.climateactionnetwork.ca.

53 See the Pew Center on Global Climate Change website (www.pewclimate.org) for comprehensive reporting on state and regional climate initiatives.

54 Kaufmann, H.R. (1990, November) "Storm damage insurance—Quo Vadis?" Swiss Re. Quoted in Leggett, J. (1993, May) "Climate Change and the Insurance Industry: Solidarity among the Risk Community?" Greenpeace. See also Linden, E. (1994, March 14) "Burned by warming." Time.

55 Ian Burton, a lead author of the April 2007 IPCC report, has said, "It's the lag effect . . . and some governments around the world are finally catching on to that point. Hitherto [climate change] has been regarded as a mitigation problem—reducing emissions." Daley, B. (2007, April 5) "US lags on plans for climate change," Boston Globe.

Appendix

56 A number of key factors seem to have brought this about, most notably: the Kyoto Protocol going into effect without U.S. ratification in February 2005; the devastation caused by Hurricane Katrina in September 2005; the success of former U.S. Vice President Al Gore's global warming film, "An Inconvenient Truth," released in May 2006; California's adoption of greenhouse gas emissions caps in August 2006; the release of the "Economics of Climate Change" by U.K. economist Sir Edward Stern in October 2006; a shift among key U.S. conservative religious groups towards accepting the need to address global warming; U.S. President George W. Bush's acknowledgement of "the serious challenge of global climate change" in his State of the Union in January 2007; and the March 2007 release of the Fourth Assessment Report of the Intergovernmental Panel of Climate Change.

57 Daley, B. (2007, April 5) "US lags on plans for climate change," Boston Globe.

58 The April 2007 conference of the American Planning Association included a special double-session devoted to exploring this continuing development in the planning field. The sessions took as their starting point the need for prioritizing urban and ecological resilience in planning and infrastructure investment planning as evidenced by the devastation wrought by Hurricane Katrina in September 2005.

59 *Soft path analysis*: Lovins, A. (1977) "Soft Energy Paths: Toward a Durable Peace." Cambridge, Massachusetts: Ballinger/Friends of the Earth; and
Brandes, O. Brooks, D. (2005) "The Soft Path for Water In a Nutshell." Ottawa: Friends of the Earth Canada / Victoria, BC: POLIS Project on Ecological Governance.
Factor Four: Weizsäcker, E., et al. (1997) "Factor Four: Doubling Wealth, Halving Resource Use." London: Earthscan. http://www.wupperinst.org/FactorFour.
Ecological Design: Van der Ryn, S. and Cowan, S. (1996) "Ecological Design" Washington, DC: Island Press.
The Natural Step: See http://www.thenaturalstep.com.

60 United Nations World Population Prospects, 2004; see http://esa.un.org/unpp.

61 ICLEI was founded as International Council for Local Environmental Initiatives, but is now known as ICLEI-Local Governments for Sustainability. Their Cities for Climate Protection five-milestone framework is the largest program working with cities around the world to track and reduce local greenhouse gas emissions. In Canada, this program is implemented for ICLEI by the Federation of Canadian Municipalities as "Partners for Climate Change"; see http://www.iclei.org.

62 Special thanks to Stuart Ramsey, Transportation Planner at the City of Burnaby, B.C., for putting this so bluntly.

63 "Zero energy buildings" are, generally speaking, buildings that produce at least as much energy as they consume. See http://www.eere.energy.gov/buildings/building_america, http://zeroenergybuilding.org, and http://www.zedfactory.com.

64 Industrial symbiosis is an industrial management practice in which the waste output of one process becomes a resource input for a different process, generating significant cost savings. It can take highly complex forms, involving materials, energy, and multiple firms. See http://www.is4ie.org.

65 Pacala, S. and Socolow, R. (2004, August 13) "Stabilization Wedges: Solving the Climate Problem for the next 50 Years with Current Technologies." Science. 305:5686 (968-972).

66 In 2006 James Hansen, director of NASA's Goddard Institute for Space Studies, set a timeline of "at most ten years" to make the changes necessary to keep global warming from reaching 2° Celsius over pre-industrial levels, warmer than the Earth has been in a million years. Hansen, J. (2006, July 13) "The Threat to the Planet," *New York Review of Books*. See also Dr. Hansen's presentation at the February 2007 "2010 Imperative" international webcast design teach-in at http://www.2010imperative.org.

67 See James, S. and Lahti, T. (2004) "The Natural Step for Communities: How Cities and Towns Can Change to Sustainable Practices." Gabriola Island, BC: New Society; information online at http://www.sjamesassociates.com/ecomunic.htm.

Photo Credits

Cover, Windmill and bridge at Exhibition Place, Toronto, Reimar Gaertner

Page i, Windmill at Exhibition Place, Toronto, Randy Park

Page ii, City Hall, Portland, Oregon, Cosmonaut Creative Media LLC

Page iii, Portland Streetcar, Portland, Oregon, Daniel Lerch

Page 1, Refinery panoramic, Jason Verschoor

Page 3, Harbor of Vancouver, Canada, Klaas Lingbeek- van Kranen

Page 7, Oil derrick at sunset, Hazlan Abdul Hakim

Page 8, Crowded highway, Tony Tremblay

Page 11, Oil pump jack, Karl Naundorf

Page 14, Natural gas storage facility, Loic Bernard

Page 15, Tar sands excavation, Alberta, Canada, Pembina Institute

Page 17, Gas station prices sign, Jose Gil

Page 21, Southwestern U.S. City Hall, Craig Barhorst

Page 24, Aerial view of highway cloverleaf, Teun van den Dries

Page 25, Aerial view of oil refinery, Edward Todd

Page 29, View of Montreal from Jacques Cartier Bridge, Tony Tremblay

Page 31, State capitol, Madison, Wisconsin, David Raboin

Page 32, Lone Buffalo on Plain, Rob Freeman

Page 35, American Dogwood, Steven Bourelle

Page 37, Spare gas tank on highway, Sascha Burkard

Page 39, Multnomah County building ecoroof, Portland Office of Sustainable Development

Page 40, Light rail train at Portland Saturday Market, Sarah Syed

Page 44, Downtown Hamilton, Ontario, City of Hamilton

Page 46, Willits arch over Highway 101, City of Willits

Page 51, Downtown New Orleans after Hurricane Katrina, September 2005, Joseph Nickischer

Page 59, Windmill and bridge at Exhibition Place, Toronto, Reimar Gaertner / Grapheon Communications Design

Page 63, Portland Streetcar, Portland, Oregon, Daniel Lerch

Page 65, Church spire and buildings, Portland, Oregon, Daniel Lerch

Page 66, Saturday Market fountain, Portland, Oregon, Sarah Syed

Page 79, Alsatian landscape, Jean Schweitzer

Index

adaptive management, 33, 35, 55, 77, 86

Alberta, Canada, 8, 14-15, 31

Anderson, Rocky, 60

asphalt, 4, 23, 25-26, 80

Austin (Texas), 38, 49

Australia, 52, 55-56

biodiesel (see biofuel)

biofuel, 3, 7, 14, 16, 22, 37, 54, 60

Birk, Mia, 30, 33

Bloomington (Indiana), 38, 49, 70, 73

buildings or built structures, 5, 8, 17, 27-28, 30, 34, 39-40, 43-45, 52-54, 60, 63, 65-66, 86-87

Burkholder, Rex, 28, 39-40, 61

Burnaby (British Columbia), 38, 47, 70, 85

Canada, 3, 8-9, 14, 24-28, 30-32, 34, 44, 52, 55, 60-62, 67, 87-90

Carbon Mitigation Initiative (see Pacala, S. or Socolow, R.)

carbon, 3, 5, 15, 28, 39, 52, 59, 60, 62, 64-65, 67, 71-72, 91

mitigation (see climate change, mitigation)

Chevron (oil company), 2, 11, 13, 15

China, 2, 10-11,15

Cities for Climate Protection Campaign (see ICLEI)

climate change

    adaptation, 51, 55-57

    effects of, 3, 4, 5, 51, 55-57

    mitigation, 38, 51-55, 62, 72

    responding to, 27, 29, 30, 33, 35, 38, 39, 41, 51-57, 59-67, 83, 85, 88-89

    climate uncertainty, 1, 3, 4, 5, 27, 29, 30, 33, 35, 41, 51, 59-67, 83, 85

Clinton Climate Initiative, 52, 88

coal, 8, 9, 15, 71

combined heating and power (CHP), 60, 65

complexity, 22, 33, 35, 83

construction (see buildings)

Cool Counties Climate Stabilization Declaration, 52

Corrigan, Derek, 63, 77

Davidson, Bryn, 64-65

dependence, energy/oil/natural gas (see vulnerability, energy/oil/natural gas)

district heating, 34

economy

    global, 2, 3, 10, 17, 19, 21, 75

    local, 28, 30-31, 60, 63, 65-67, 74-76, 80-81

elected officials (see government officials)

emergency services/response/plan, 5, 27, 43, 57, 74-76

Energy Information Administration (EIA), 10, 12-13, 90

energy

    consumption/demand, 8, 14, 23, 28, 38, 41, 43, 46, 49, 59, 64-65, 74, 79

    efficiency, 18, 28-29, 31, 34, 39, 43, 45, 51-55, 60-61, 64-65, 67, 85, 87

    embodied, 3

    independence, 35, 38, 70, 85, 88

    price, 21, 35, 43, 46, 48, 64, 70

    renewable/alternative, 16-17, 29, 34, 39, 46, 48, 54, 60-61, 71, 87

    returned on invested (EROI), 14

    security, 2, 57, 71

    uncertainty, 2-5, 21-22, 27, 29-30, 33, 35, 37, 41, 50, 59-67, 70, 78, 83

ethanol (see biofuel)

Europe, 14, 27, 34, 56, 61, 77

European Union, 3, 14, 55

ExxonMobil (oil company), 13

Factor Four, 61

Falleri, Alan, 35, 50, 70

Federation of Canadian Municipalities, 32, 87-88

fertilizer, 3, 8, 15-16

food, 2-3, 5, 8-9, 15-16, 22-23, 39-41, 43, 48, 55, 59-60, 67, 71, 74, 76-77, 86, 90

Ford, Patrick, 22

Franklin (New York), 38

fuel (see energy)

geothermal, 9, 17, 86

global warming (see climate change)

government

    officials, 5, 21, 27, 29, 31-33, 37, 41, 45-47, 49-51, 60-61, 63, 65, 67, 70, 72-74, 79, 85, 87-89

    local, 1, 4-5, 8, 21-22, 24-30, 32-33, 37-57, 60-63, 67, 70-77, 79-89

    role of, 3-5, 8, 17-19, 21, 27-30, 33

Great Plains, 32

green building, 22, 34, 39, 44, 54, 61

Gulf of Mexico, 10, 11, 14, 15, 25

Hamilton (Ontario), 38, 44-45, 72, 85

Heinberg, Richard, 10, 49

Hickenlooper, John, 40

Hirsch Report, 12, 18

Hubbert Curve, 11

Hurricane Katrina, 4, 10, 25, 27, 51

Index

hydrocarbons (see carbon)

hydrogen, 8, 16

hydropower, 9, 17

ICLEI, Cities for Climate Protection Campaign, 46, 52-53, 61-62, 85-86, 88-89

Intergovernmental Panel on Climate Change, 51, 55-56

International Energy Agency (IEA), 9-12, 85

Iran, 2, 10-12, 14, 16

Iraq, 10

Japan, 15, 34

Kansas, 32

Kyoto Protocol, 51, 52, 54, 62

land use, 1, 5, 21-24, 27-31, 34, 39-41, 43-44, 57, 60-61, 63, 74-77, 85, 86, 90

leadership, 19, 28, 30, 32-33, 43, 50, 63

Liquefied Natural Gas (LNG; see natural gas)

local government (see government, local)

localization (see relocalization)

manufacturing, local, 60, 67

market(s), economic, 2-4, 7, 9-11, 17, 19, 54, 71, 87-88, 90

McKibben, Bill, 7

Metro (regional government of Portland, Oregon), 38-42, 72

Montreal Declaration (see World Mayors and Municipal Leaders Declaration)

municipalities (see government, local)

natural gas

    consumption (see energy, consumption)

    price of, 7, 14-16, 22, 75, 79

    supply of, 2, 5, 7-8, 14-17, 22, 27, 32-33, 64, 71, 74

    uses of, 3, 8-9, 14-16, 23, 75

Natural Step, The, 61, 77, 83, 86

Nelessen, Anton, 62

net metering, 34

New Urbanism, 34

New Zealand, 57

Nickels, Greg, 52, 54

Nigeria, 10

North America, 14, 17, 35, 55-56, 61, 71

North Carolina, 4, 27, 87

North Sea, 11

Norway, 14

nuclear power, 8-9, 16, 34

O'Neill, Beverly, 21

Oakland (California), 38

Oil Depletion Protocol, 41, 49, 61, 71

oil

    alternatives to, substitutes for, 2-3, 7, 14-18, 29, 34, 39, 46, 48, 55, 60, 61, 87

    consumption (see energy, consumption)

    deep-sea or deepwater, 11, 15

    demand for, 2-3, 9-13, 25-26, 17-19, 70, 85

    dependence on (see vulnerability, energy/oil/natural gas)

    flow, 10-11, 17

    non-conventional or unconventional, 11, 14-15

    peak or peaking (see peak oil)

    polar, 15

    price and price volatility, 1-5, 7-8, 10-11, 13-15, 17-19, 22, 24-26, 28-29, 37, 39, 47, 49, 62-63, 67, 71, 73-77, 79

    production, 1-2, 5, 7, 9-14, 18-19, 23, 25, 34, 40, 47, 62, 67, 70-71

    shale, 15

    supply of, 2, 7, 9-13, 17-19, 32-33, 64, 70, 74

    uses of, 3, 8-9, 16, 75

Orenstein, Ron, 46

Pacala, Stephen, 64-65

peak natural gas (see peak oil)

Peak Oil Task Force, 22-23, 38, 40-43, 50, 62, 73-78, 85

peak oil, 1-5, 7-13, 17-18, 21-23, 32-33, 37-47, 49-50, 59-63, 65, 67, 70-77, 85, 90

petroleum (see oil)

photovoltaic cells (see solar power)

Popper, Deborah, 32

Popper, Frank, 32

Portland (Oregon), 22, 30, 38-43, 50, 72-73, 78

    Peak Oil Task Force, 22-23, 38-43, 46, 50, 73, 76, 78, 85

Post Carbon Institute, 67, 85

private sector, 4, 37, 56-57, 63, 65, 71

public services, 1, 3, 5, 21-23, 28-31, 38-41, 44, 46-48, 57, 79

Ramsey, Stuart, 47

Rees, William, 59

relocalization, 38, 59, 67

resilience, 5, 55, 66-67, 81-84

risk or risk management, 1-2, 4-5, 10, 16, 18, 21, 23, 27-29, 38, 41, 48, 51, 55-57, 74-76, 88

Robinson, Larry, 47

Rollo, Dave, 22, 49, 73

Russia, 2, 10, 14

Saltzman, Dan, 40

San Francisco (California), 38, 70-71

Saudi Arabia, 2, 10-12, 15

Seattle (Washington), 52, 54

Sebastopol (California), 38, 47-48, 50, 78

    Citizens Advisory Group on Energy Vulnerability, 78, 85

Smart Growth, 30, 34, 86, 89

Spokane (Washington), 38, 49

Socolow, Robert, 64-65

soft path analysis, 61

solar power, 7, 9, 17, 22, 34, 38, 44, 46, 48, 54, 60, 86

South America, 27

Southern California Association of Governments, 38

State Energy Offices, 31, 87

street maintenance, 4, 23, 25-26, 30, 74, 80-82

sustainable development, 34, 49, 51, 83

system(s) or systems thinking, 4, 17, 29, 35, 55, 60, 75, 77, 79-84, 86

tar sands, 7, 11, 15

Texas, 14-15

transit-oriented development, 30, 34

transportation, 1-2, 4-5, 8-9, 17-18, 21-25, 28-32, 34, 39-41, 43-44, 46-48, 54, 60-61, 63, 74-77, 80-81, 86-87, 89-90

U.S. Conference of Mayors, 32, 52, 54, 85, 88

U.S. Mayors Climate Protection Agreement, 52, 54, 61-62, 85, 89

uncertainty (see energy uncertainty or climate uncertainty)

United States, 1, 5, 8-9, 14, 31, 34, 51-52, 62, 67, 83, 87-89

uranium, 16

Venezuela, 2, 10-11, 14-15

vulnerability, 1-2, 4-5, 21-23, 25, 27, 29-30, 33, 37-38, 41, 46-50, 55-56, 62-63, 65, 67, 70, 73-78, 85

    specific to energy/oil/natural gas, 1-5, 9-11, 14, 17-19, 22-23, 25-30, 33, 38, 41, 47-50, 62-63, 65, 67, 70, 73, 75, 77

wedge strategies, 64, 65

Willits (California), 38, 46, 50, 77, 85

Willits Economic Localization (WELL), 46, 85

wind power, 7, 9, 17, 34, 45, 48, 54, 60, 86

World Mayors and Municipal Leaders Declaration on Climate Change, 52, 61-62